space
WITHIN

space
WITHIN

Reshaping the **home** for contemporary living

Jane Withers   Photographs by Christoph Kicherer

Quadrille

Editorial Director: Anne Furniss
Creative Director: Mary Evans
Consultant Art Director: Helen Lewis
Project Editor: Hilary Mandleberg
Production: Sarah Tucker
Picture Research: Nadine Bazar
Picture Assistant: Sarah Airey
Plans: Richard Blurton and Patrick McKinney

First published in 2000 by
Quadrille Publishing Limited
Alhambra House
27–31 Charing Cross Road
London WC2H 0LS

This paperback edition published in 2002

British Library Cataloguing-in-Publication Data
A catalogue record for this book is available from
the British Library.

ISBN 1 903845 58 0

Printed and bound in Singapore

Contents

Introduction

One of the problems we face in designing living spaces today may be less to do with how we want to live and more to do with how we negotiate a way between what exists and the kind of space we want to inhabit. In many densely populated cities, where the built heritage far outweighs the possibilities of new building, we are less likely to live in a home purpose built to suit a contemporary way of life than to be forced to work deftly within the constraints of existing buildings, subverting and reinventing them to meet new needs and desires.

The centre of practically any city over a certain age illustrates how far-reaching this process of recycling buildings has become. The conflicting forces of conservation and the desire to modernise, constraints on space and strict planning laws – all have helped make schizophrenia a part of everyday urban experience. A fast-food joint inserted into a Victorian shop front or a Georgian interior muffled in corporate ceiling tiles and strip lighting hardly raise an eyebrow. But in the residential arena, too, extraordinary and sometimes incongruous juxtapositions are becoming more commonplace as houses built to serve a very different world from our own are dramatically reconfigured for contemporary living, and industrial, commercial and institutional buildings are colonised for residential use. Behind the strict uniformity of a terrace we find the niceties of dining room and front parlour have been replaced by loft-scaled living rooms. Inside industrial buildings, instead of grimy sweat-stained workshops, we find bleached white interiors on the scale of hotel lobbies. Sometimes all that is left of the original building is its façade.

Of course this isn't an altogether new phenomenon. It could be argued that house interiors through history have been modified to keep up with new trends in decoration and convenience. Yet increasingly, refurbishing domestic interiors is becoming not just about updating decoration but about radical spatial reorganisation.

All sorts of social, economic and cultural conditions are behind this, as housing struggles to keep up to date with dynamic changes in society. In the catalogue accompanying a recent exhibition at the Museum of Modern Art, New York, 'The Un-Private House', curator Terence Riley observes: 'The social conditions and structures that drove the development of the private house – privacy, the separation of living and work, the family, domesticity – have all changed drastically, perhaps more so in the last fifty years than in the preceding four centuries.'

The design of the majority of homes could once be securely based on the structure and needs of the nuclear family, but housing is increasingly forced to adapt to suit the multiplicity of society and more transitory lifestyles. At the same time, new communications and information technologies are altering the relationship between the home and the outside world and between private and working lives.

This state of uncertainty is reflected in the shift towards homes that, rather than reinforcing a particular way of life, are designed to accommodate change. Just how far out of sync the contemporary way of inhabiting the home is with the residential structures we have inherited is revealed by the problems we encounter in giving names to the rooms we live in.

A hundred years ago, rooms could safely be named by function – parlour, dining room, even drawing room – and the number and complexity of the subdivisions reflected the wealth of the household. In less structured living spaces, such labels have become increasingly redundant and the popularity of loft living has helped make talk of living spaces, areas and even zones common currency – but this can easily slip into pretension.

The homes included here have been chosen to highlight different ways in which existing structures can be adapted to suit contemporary living patterns. Projects range from a 60sq. m. (650sq. yd.) studio to a substantial suburban villa, from robust solutions which make creative use of limited resources, to the luxuriously budgeted, from family homes to single-person units. Yet in their commitment to responding to new ways of living, their questioning of the present and their attempts at foreseeing the future, they reveal more universal concerns.

In the past, individual architect-designed homes or refurbishments were mostly the province of a wealthy elite or the design-literate, and to some extent this is still true. Even if it is a renovation, a custom-designed home is a complex synthesis of spatial planning, cost-efficiency and aesthetic, and requires commitment and imagination on the part of both client and architect. Yet the extent to which we are forced to work with old structures makes the clever architect's ability to find imaginative and unorthodox solutions to unlock the potential in a building vital.

But the home is much more than a giant inhabited sculpture: it has to function on many levels. As well as being a physical shelter, it is an intimate psychological environment. The history of the plan of the home reads like a map of changing social relations within the household. In the medieval home, the lack of formal divisions reflected a way of life where privacy was virtually non-existent. By the nineteenth century, the rigid corsetry of the cellular room plan reinforced the patriarchal hierarchy of the Victorian family. Architectural historian Robin Evans goes so far as to suggest that the corridor plan which, by the nineteenth century, had replaced the matrix of interconnecting rooms of earlier, more gregarious households, reflected a society 'that finds carnality distasteful, which sees the body as a vessel of mind and spirit, and in which privacy is habitual'.

The generalised shift towards increasingly open-plan living spaces took shape with the pioneering Modernists' radical re-examination of the home. Writing on 'The Dwelling as a Problem', in 1930, Finnish architect Alvar Aalto railed against the tyranny of the room: 'A dwelling is an area which should offer protected areas for meals, sleep, work and play. These biodynamic functions should be taken as points of departure for the dwelling's internal division, not any outdated symmetrical axis or "standard room" dictated by façade architecture.'

Lofts have also done a lot to popularise flexible multi-purpose living spaces, shifting in fifty years from the radical Bohemian fringe to become a mainstream housing option. Ironically, developers even build new loft buildings, erecting mock factory- or warehouse-style buildings for domestic use.

At first, the loft – the home as container bounded only by its walls – offered the freedom of a space without frontiers, a home without preconceptions that we can occupy and alter as we like. Yet total open plan has turned out to have constrictions of its own and just as we remove walls in houses and apartments, so we install internal divisions in lofts, although not necessarily in the form of conventional rooms. 'Residential structures will be focusing on a more hybrid condition,' observes architect Zaha Hadid. 'Walled-off rooms with strictly defined functions will not be able to accommodate a society where gender-defined roles and forms of parenting dissolve and become more fluid. The future home will be a more integrated, inclusive space which will ease the free flow from work to child-care to meals, etc. Instead of separation, there will be differentiated terrain where furniture takes on the role of defining elements.'

Many of the homes featured here illustrate this layering – even interweaving – of different territories, the communal and the private, the open and the intimate, the shared and the personal, depending on the make-up of the household.

It has been argued that in breaking down the strictures of the room, we are going back to a way of life more familiar to the Middle Ages than to the last four hundred or so years. In the medieval home, pretty much all activities took place in one room. The table was used for eating and entertaining, for business and counting money. The same room often accommodated day and night quarters with, at most, a bed enclosed in an alcove.

In *Home: A Short History of an Idea*, architect and historian Witold Rybczynski describes how, from the seventeenth century onwards, with increasing prosperity, the home began to be planned not only to accommodate separate day and night quarters, but to divorce cooking from eating, and to move work into the separate domain of the office and factory. By the mid-nineteenth century, the home was established as a private world, a counterpoint to public life. This, it could be argued, is the structure we are in the process of dismantling today.

How and where we prepare food and eat have changed dramatically. Not only has the dining room almost disappeared from the daily domestic vocabulary in all but the most formal houses, but the preparation of food is once again associated with eating, and the kitchen has shifted from being a service adjunct to become the sociable epicentre of many contemporary homes.

Given the growth in pre-prepared and takeaway foods and eating out, this symbolic elevation of the kitchen is rather ironic, but perhaps no more incongruous than 4 x 4 vehicles designed for forging rivers and scaling cliffs being used on the school run. In Manhattan in the 1980s, at the height of the yuppie boom, one developer observed the lifestyle of urban professionals who even ordered in breakfast rather than brew coffee at home, and in response designed apartments without kitchens. But the experiment was quickly dropped. Rather like the open hearth in a centrally heated home, the kitchen may be as much a symbolic emblem of warmth and nourishment as an actual place of food preparation.

Rybczynski argues that the emergence of the servantless household was probably more important in shaping the modern home than any technological developments. As the housewife took over from the housekeeper, the modern kitchen began to take shape from what was a haphazard conglomeration of furniture and unwieldy domestic appliances. Since then, the kitchen has ridden the roller-coaster of fashion, from diner to loose-fitted farmhouse kitchen, from high-tech fuelling station to industrial stainless steel.

French designer Andrée Putman rates the kitchen and bathroom together in terms of their importance in satisfying our spiritual and emotional needs and bringing an elemental presence to the home that is often lacking in modern urban lives. 'I believe the closest attention should always be paid to the bathroom and the kitchen, the seat of fire and water, where the ancient and laughable drama of human life is played out, interspersed by the repeated actions of using water for washing and fire for cooking. This would ensure that these rooms offer the vital level of physical comfort essential for our spiritual ease.'

Just as the kitchen has been reinvented, so something similar is beginning to happen to the bathroom. For much of the twentieth century, in the West at least, bathing has been constrained by the hangover of Victorian prudery and the early Modernist cult of physical and mental health. Purpose-built bathrooms were generally small, functional and bleak, and more attuned to clinical correctness than to sensuality and pleasure.

Today, the increasing attention given to bathing is reflected in the space allotted to it. It is now not unusual to devote a room on the scale of a bedroom to bathing. Equally, bathing is sometimes integrated into the home in unexpected ways, reflecting increasingly relaxed attitudes to sexuality, while materials are chosen for their tactile and sensual as well as their practical and hygienic qualities.

Certain contemporary designers are looking to non-Western bathing traditions, such as the extra-ordinarily refined Japanese bathing culture, the Scandinavian sauna tradition or the Turkish bath. In these, bathing environments keep pace with technological developments without being desensitised in the way that has happened in the West, and the enjoyment and celebration of water are as important as the physical process of cleansing.

Domestic technology is now at an interesting point. While experimental architects have intrigued, entertained and disquieted the public with visions of futuristic habitats, whose walls and floors take on the character of chameleons and where virtual chefs materialise like genies in the kitchen, by and large, the fabric of most homes and the basic domestic services and technologies remain remarkably conventional. As industry standards are agreed, the connected home, where appliances and services will be able to communicate with each other, is becoming a reality. This will make the home not only more automated, but capable of being customised to suit individual preferences. Yet what effect this will have on the planning and fabric of the home remains to be seen. As many of the homes here illustrate, we may desire a domestic environment that at least appears to be a counterpoint to the wired urban world.

Certainly though, with new digital media, the home is becoming less like a retreat and more like a giant communications console that can receive and transmit information and images, sound and data from and to the entire world. Yet the real shifts may be as much psychological and behavourial as physical.

Potentially one of the most far-reaching effects of this on the home is on the work front. The vision of a society of knowledge workers tapping away at home in their pyjamas while linked to the world via new communications has failed to materialise as surely as the confident prediction that technology would liberate us from the 40-hour working week and deliver us into a leisure society. Instead, IT is increasingly blurring the boundaries between our home and work lives, eroding the nine-to-five working day and making work a presence in many homes, although not necessarily in the home office. As technology finally begins to make the 'work anywhere any time' mantra of the 1990s feasible, it is possible for many of us to work in more informal and nomadic ways, inside and outside the home, discreetly supported by technology rather than tied to a conventional office environment.

As cyberspace becomes a powerful alternative to the real world and homes adjust to this, Californian architect Wes Jones proposes that the digital revolution will have far-reaching social effects. Cyberspace 'will challenge the cohesiveness of the family as children become self-sufficient citizens of the virtual world . . . As the family becomes more diffuse, the home would be expected to take on more the character of an apartment building, with each member having their own "unit" – except that such physical niceties will not be seen as very important any longer.' According to Jones, the home will be organised to accommodate 'individual past time areas, primarily surfing-related, and community areas', and the family room will become 'a non virtual *agora* for those who crave an old-fashioned encounter with a relative.'

Whether such a chilling vision of a society fragmented by the schism between the virtual and the real will materialise remains to be seen. Yet there is no doubt that such forces are beginning to affect the character of the domestic environment. For all these reasons, design is one of the most significant ways in which we can shape our own domestic world and achieve homes that fulfil our needs and desires within the carcasses of existing buildings.

House by Rachel Whiteread, 1993.

Town House

RIGHT *A Woman Drinking with Two Men, and a Serving Woman, c.1658,* by Pieter de Hooch. De Hooch's paintings illustrate life in the seventeenth-century Dutch town house. The main living room, lofty and austerely furnished with a table used for dining, entertaining and business, is not so very different from the informality of how we live today.

Whether one thinks of Manhattan's brooding brownstones, the austere Georgian terraces of Dublin, Bath or Edinburgh, London's white stucco squares or the crenelated red-brick houses lining Amsterdam's canals, one sees that the town house has been one of the principal building blocks of cities around the world, and still remains an urban ideal today.

Although it might seem to be a residential model rooted in the habitation patterns of another age, and its rigid corsetry and vertical stack of rooms might appear to be opposed to our increasing move towards more lateral, open and flexible living spaces, it has proved a surprisingly durable residential model. Already most town houses have lasted considerably longer than their builders would have expected and in these conservation-minded times, they look likely to continue. At the same time, the density of habitation that can be achieved with town houses means that they are still a feasible model for building.

The uniformity of the typical town-house façade may give the impression of inflexibility, but paradoxically it is this that has contributed to the town house's longevity. The façade often has an independent existence from the interior, which may have been regularly altered to bring it up to date with contemporary ideas of convenience and comfort. Today's more extreme conversions, which sometimes retain little of the original house other than the foundations and the façade, may seem almost schizophrenic, presenting one character to the street and reserving another for interior life, but there is little new about this.

With the Place des Vosges, the elegant Parisian square created by Henri IV after his entry into Paris in 1594, the aristocracy abandoned the custom of living in *hôtels particuliers* – private houses set back from

the street and arranged around a courtyard – to build town houses whose rooms look directly onto the square and where each façade is identical to its neighbours. But while the deeds imposed uniformity on the façade, behind that people could build what they liked. This concept of 'façadism' also existed from early on in the London town house. In some districts, new terraces of family houses were in fact carved into flats or rooms near the outset of their lives. Thus there is nothing new about problems such as inadequate soundproofing that we find today in flats converted from houses. In Slim House, Pierre d'Avoine's competition-winning concept for a contemporary reinterpretation of the traditional small terraced house, d'Avoine plays on this characteristic. Slim House's façade is little more than a billboard, presenting an orderly front to the street while allowing individual inhabitants to arrange their own interiors.

The town house has it origins in medieval cities, where the pressure on space in fortified towns brought about high land values, dense building on narrow plots and upward development. An extreme version of this can still be seen in the extraordinary mud skyscrapers of the Yemen. The town of Shibalm in the south is known as the Manhattan of the desert, after its crenelated skyline, where towers rise as high as nine storeys. The town grew up to protect the trade routes from the Middle East to North Africa. The high value of irrigated land for cultivation in this desert oasis is what forced this extreme upwards development.

A more familiar history of the town house can be traced in the houses that front the canals of Amsterdam. Because of the canal layout, the medieval Dutch house was built on a narrow plot and usually consisted of a single-storey dwelling built over a cellar used for storage. Initially, such houses combined

An illustration from a Dutch fire-fighters' instruction manual of 1690 shows a typical large town house. The raised ground floor has the main living room at the back while the central spiral wooden staircase leads to the bedrooms on the first floor and the laundry above. The basement is used for storage.

living and working, and the interior was often divided into two: a front room where commercial activities took place – usually either a shop or workshop – and behind this, the living quarters, where the whole panoply of daily – and night – life took place, not in a series of rooms but in one big chamber.

In *Home: A Short History of an Idea*, author Witold Rybczinski describes how in seventeenth-century Holland, the town house – and home life more or less as we know it – began to take shape. Prosperous burghers in the newly formed United Provinces of the Netherlands, which has been described as the first bourgeois state, extended their embryonic town houses in the only direction possible – upwards. The first addition was often a gallery or loft space, and further floors were added after this.

According to Rybczynski, 'Initially, these rooms, with the exception of the kitchen, did not have special functions. By mid-century, however, the subdivision of the house into day and night uses, and into formal and informal areas, had begun.' With increasing prosperity, work was removed from the house as those who could afford it built separate business establishments, thus initiating the town house as a family home.

Another aspect of the Dutch house was the private garden at the back. Whereas the typical continental town houses of this period were organised around a communal courtyard that was essentially a public space, the Dutch house generally had a stoop or verandah at the front and a secluded rear garden.

The eighteenth century is acknowledged as a high point in town-house architecture in England and set the scene for the American rowhouses. While there is huge variety in the scale and plan of these houses, stretching from the artisan's modest terrace to the elegant grandeur of the houses of the nobility, by the mid-eighteenth century, the middle ground of terraced town house evolved into a fairly standard plan.

In *The Complete Body of Architecture* of 1755, Isaac Ware describes the Common House as being three windows wide with a basement and four storeys, including a garret, above this and with a dog-leg staircase in the rear corner. Generally, there were three rooms, including the rear closet wing, on each principal floor. Chimney stacks were accommodated in the party wall with one fireplace heating each main room.

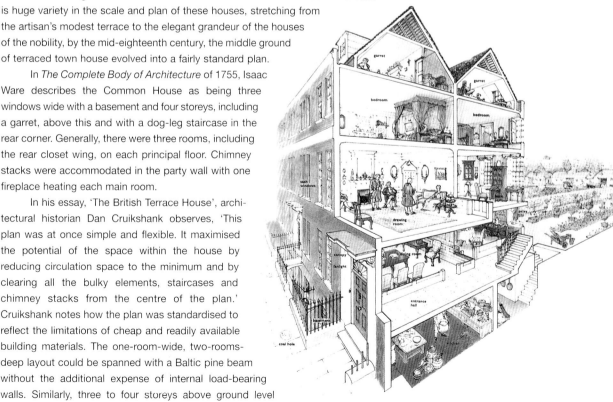

In his essay, 'The British Terrace House', architectural historian Dan Cruikshank observes, 'This plan was at once simple and flexible. It maximised the potential of the space within the house by reducing circulation space to the minimum and by clearing all the bulky elements, staircases and chimney stacks from the centre of the plan.' Cruikshank notes how the plan was standardised to reflect the limitations of cheap and readily available building materials. The one-room-wide, two-rooms-deep layout could be spanned with a Baltic pine beam without the additional expense of internal load-bearing walls. Similarly, three to four storeys above ground level could be built without substantial foundations.

In a typical London home of a gentleman and his family *c.*1750, the hall and staircase are designed to make an impressive approach to the drawing room on the first floor away from street noise and dirt. The dining room is on the ground floor, and the kitchen in the basement.

The way the town house was inhabited is revealed in the hierarchy of the façade and its interior decoration. The main entertaining and living rooms were generally on the ground and first floors, and this was reflected on the façade by the use of generously scaled windows at these levels. The bedrooms were on the floors above this, and the servants' quarters above them, in the garret. The kitchen was in the basement along with additional storage rooms and possibly further servants' quarters. A late eighteenth- and nineteenth-century alteration consisted of inserting intercommunicating doors between the main entertaining rooms. Later still, with the arrival of the fixed bathroom, extensions were often added in haphazard fashion to the rear of the house.

The flexibility and durability of this interior plan was helped by factors of construction. Cruikshank describes how the construction of the English terraced house was such that the façade and interior had relative structural independence, since the shell was built of masonry, while the floors and virtually all the internal partitions were of wood and plaster. Timber girders and joists helped stabilise the structure, but as Cruikshank points out, façade and interior 'led two separate lives' with no 'external expression of the internal structure'. This meant that façades could be – and indeed often were – rebuilt to bring the structure up to date, while the interior was left untouched. Today, though, this has been reversed and we more commonly find a façade that appears to preserve the formality of another age while inside, the layout has been altered to meet new domestic needs. The stylistic disjuncture is sometimes so extraordinary that on opening the front door the visitor is shot fast forward through a couple of centuries.

Architect Richard Rogers' conversion of a pair of town houses in London's Chelsea for his own family, illustrates how far (with expertise and an extensive budget) the terraced house, or rather a pair of terraced houses, can be adapted for contemporary living. Located on the corner of Royal Avenue, the two flat-fronted 1840s houses in this stringent conservation zone look across the garden square towards Sir Christopher Wren's magnificent Chelsea Hospital. The formal white stucco façades remain identical to their neighbours, but glimpses through the window reveal Warhol's 'Chairman Mao' floating in a cavernous space – a hint that something unexpected is happening on the inside.

The two houses have been gutted and made into one by removing the party wall and replacing it with a steel support system. The original vertical thrust has effectively been replaced by lateral emphasis so that the house is divided horizontally into different living zones. The central feature, a double-height living space that spans the first and second floors of the two houses, is more like the sort of dramatic living space we might expect to find in a loft than in a terraced house. The hierarchical formality of the town house, in which the emphasis is usually on the ground and first floors where the principal entertaining rooms are to be found, tends to dictate how these floors are treated today. Here the new order means that the emphasis is on the first floor, whose mezzanine gallery takes advantage of the light and the views across the square.

While this conversion might seem to be a fairly extreme manipulation of a valuable property, it does reveal possibilities that can be exploited by those on smaller budgets. The Jeff Delsalle house (pages 52–7) is a banally ordinary 'semi' in an area of West London where urban blurs into suburban. Behind the drab pebble-dashed and half-timbered façade, the internal walls have been swept away and ceiling levels altered to make generous open-plan living quarters for a young couple. The original staircase has been replaced by an industrial metal staircase that helps considerably in creating a sense of space.

Such a shift from self-contained rooms with designated purposes towards larger, more open and flexible multi-purpose spaces, might seem characteristic of the changing emphasis in modern domestic space, but it in fact also harks back to much earlier precedents, recalling the multi-purpose living spaces of the medieval house.

In the town house, the staircase has been constantly moved around either for effect or to take up the minimum floor space. In an eighteenth-century town house in Spitalfields in London's East End, the hall runs from the front door through to the back garden.

One of the constant drives in town-house development has been to make lighter, airier rooms. Part of this drive has been as a result of the fact that, generally speaking, windows have become larger as new means have been found to handle increasingly large panes of glass safely. In the Thomas Dane maisonette on pages 42–5, the original sash windows have been replaced by four large plates of glass, turning the emphasis away from the front of the house and the street towards the garden at the back. In the Pawson house (pages 46–51), the main living area is in the basement kitchen, positioned to take advantage of the garden. At the rear, the masonry has been replaced by a glass wall dividing interior from exterior, while a long kitchen counter running the length of the interior extends to the far end of the garden, unifying indoor and outdoor living areas. In the Delsalle house, less stringent conservation laws permitted a deft alteration to the façade. Here the gable end was replaced with a triangular glass window.

The conservatory has been a fairly commonplace addition to all sorts of houses and certain contemporary extensions are able to play on the idea of a glass room without resorting to historical pastiche. In the terraced house in London's East End, refurbished by Adjaye and Russell (pages 30–37), the eating area is in a conservatory that adjoins the kitchen and roof garden. It has a fixed glass roof and an industrial window system so its glass walls can be folded back according to the weather.

In larger town houses, where rooms are more than two deep – as in Slim House, which occupies the full depth of the site – lightwells can be used to bring light into the middle of the house.

The staircase is one of the major components of the town house that has been moved around continually in order to maximise the living space and make circulation more efficient. In the conversion of his relatively small mid-nineteenth-century semi-detached terraced house, architect John Pawson estimated that in the original plan, the staircase occupied twenty-five percent of the floor space. In his redesign, a dramatically narrow and enclosed flight runs from the ground floor to the top, with a landing providing access to the first-floor bedroom and bathroom. It is lit by a slit of a skylight that recalls a way of illuminating a stairwell common in the eighteenth century but which creates a sense of tension between old and new. In the Delsalle house the old solid staircase has been replaced by industrial metal stairs that are visually much lighter. These rise directly from the living room: there is no space-consuming division of a hallway.

In the Rogers' Chelsea conversion, the new plan recalls the circulation system in larger town houses, where there was a principal staircase connecting the formal rooms, and a secondary 'service' staircase that ran from basement to garret. Here, the garden has been glassed-in to make an atrium that houses a staircase. This links the entrance with the living level and progresses through to the bedroom and bathroom on the mezzanine. A spiral staircase provides alternative access to all floors.

Another iconic reworking of the town house moves in exactly the opposite direction. Although the later American Modernist Paul Rudolph's theatrical penthouse eyrie is not strictly a conversion but an

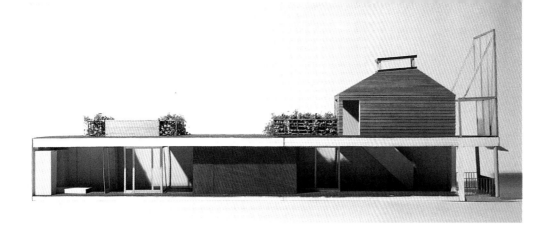

LEFT American
architect Paul
Rudolph's dramatic
penthouse extension
(1973–8) on top of
a Manhattan brown-
stone exaggerates
the vertical thrust of
the town house to
make a multi-level
maze of dramatic
spatial complexity.

audacious extension above a traditional brownstone, it shows how the vertical thrust can be taken to playful extremes. The extension, which is supported on a grid of steel beams, occupies four storeys, yet there are as many as seventeen different levels woven together around a central open space to create a vertiginous cubist composition of great spatial complexity. Rudolph's idea was to create a dynamic pin-wheeling space, where the possibility of continual movement propels visitors through a maze. Here floors are cut away to reveal voids and levels are linked by minimal stairs and perspex bridges, reflecting the architect's pre-occupation with weightlessness and transparency.

As we have seen, the terraced or town house is a building block that has been adapted, often in piecemeal fashion, to suit new ways of living and domestic requirements. Yet if it were rethought today, what would emerge? While the new-build is technically outside the scope of this book, new town-house projects are interesting because they reveal contemporary directions and ideal spatial configurations.

The most radical aspect of Slim House is that, instead of assuming each house to be a private castle with its individual garden, d'Avoine has built a long, low house over the entire plot and has raised the outdoor 'garden' space to roof level. This creates the possibility of a communal rooftop garden where residents can meet – or equally can sit glaring at each other from their own fenced-off areas. This recalls not only the communal roof spaces of utopian Modernist schemes, but also the way that the street in front of workers' terraced housing was once used as a place for children to play and parents to gossip. As the increase of cars has made this impractical in most urban developments, the idea of elevating a pedestrian 'street' above the level of traffic and fumes is an attractive concept.

Another important aspect of the traditional terrace that d'Avoine retains is that of a uniform street frontage that is almost independent of the interior, allowing residents the flexibility for each house to have its own plan and character and be adapted to different domestic needs. Behind the standard façade, the house can be extended by the addition of a third storey and it can also encompass open-plan and double-height living areas. D'Avoine's plan also allows space for working at home. Harking back to the precedent of early town houses, before work was separated from home life, he proposes that his plan might even encompass a small, family-run shop or workshop at the front.

As well as being intelligently organised and socially optimistic, Slim House could also be economic. The rules of the competition of which Slim House was the winner dictated that the house be for mass production and should cost £45,000 – pretty much in line with what developers spend on a similar-sized house.

The raised garden, where planning allows, is an intelligent adaptation of the town house to suit contemporary urban conditions. In the terraced house by Trevor Horne on pages 38–41, the ground floor originally contained a shop, which has been turned into a furniture gallery, while the light industrial building built over the garden area is now used as a painting studio. The studio roof serves as a lawned terrace accessible at first-floor level. Similarly, in the former artisan's house in Spitalfields converted by Adjaye and Russell (pages 30–37), the ground floor has been extended into the garden to make a substantial studio with a terrace on the roof adjoining the kitchen area. In the Belgian town house (pages 22–9), the entrance hall provides access to living quarters upstairs and the office on the ground floor, providing a degree of separation between home and work life. Where many town-house gardens have been made dark and dingy by surrounding buildings, raising the 'garden' provides the possibility of reclaiming a light outdoor area, safely removed from street level, while also extending the built space.

ABOVE Slim House,
designed by Pierre
d'Avoine, is a
proposal for a
contemporary
re-working of the
town house in which
the façade is little
more than a billboard
enabling the living
accommodation to
be arranged behind
it to suit individual
requirements. The
built area extends
over the whole plot
with the garden raised
to first-floor level.

A rear extension transforms a small
Belgian town house from a conventional stack of
small rooms to a home filled with unexpected
light and space

At the front, the town house has been preserved, including alterations to the façade that remain from an earlier conversion.

At the rear, the modern extension has a double-height living space and terrace above.

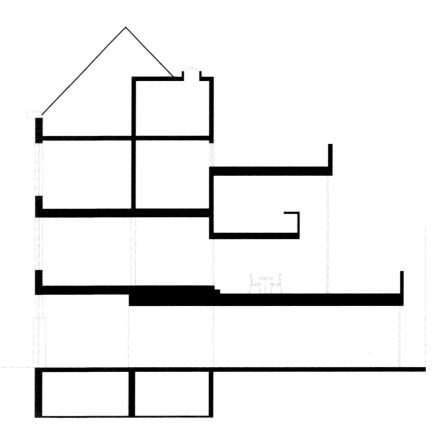

PREVIOUS PAGE **With its 6m. (20ft.) glass doors that open so the dining area extends onto the terrace, the rear extension provides a total contrast to the original house.**

ABOVE (left and right) **The entrance hall acts as a holding bay for visitors to home and office. A wall at the back slides to the right to reveal the slightly askew wooden staircase, and to the left to lead into the ground-floor office.**

OPPOSITE **The original wooden stairs provide a circulation space between the old and new buildings.**

The problem faced in the conversion of this utterly ordinary town house in Antwerp was principally one of size. Dating from the early twentieth century, the original house, only 3.8m. (12ft. 6in.) wide, consisted of a stack of relatively small rooms. In Belgian architect Vincent van Duysen's transformation, a muscular rear extension creates an unexpectedly spacious counterpoint to the original house.

Designed to accommodate an office for the owner's modern furniture business as well as a home for her and her elderly mother, the house has been altered by van Duysen to reflect the owner's emotional attachment to the house where she grew up. Instead of eradicating or disguising the old structure, one of its elements, the original wooden staircase, has been deliberately preserved, even celebrated. Connecting the old and new buildings, the endearingly wonky stairs have been turned into a sort of spinal column, the pivot of the redesign both from an aesthetic point of view and an organisational one. As well as providing a link between the stripped-down interior of the original house and the cleaner, rectilinear extension, the exposed staircase adds an element of tactile roughness that is characteristic of van Duysen's design and is sometimes missing from more clinically minimal interiors.

In the modern extension, van Duysen uses glass extensively to make the new rooms as light as possible. A ground-floor rear extension houses the office, with a small patio behind to let in light. Above this, the emphatic structure frames a double-height living area with 6m. (20ft.) high glass doors that allow it to open onto the terrace. Inside, a dining area occupies the lower level and above that are a mezzanine library and sitting area.

On the next floor, at bedroom level, the extension has a second terrace. The concrete framework is intended to create a feeling of privacy and protection, away from the distractions of the city and focusing on contemplative views of the sky.

The original stairs have now evolved into a service core, which, as well as connecting the old and the new, also houses sanitary facilities and storage and serves the rooms at both front and rear.

One of the problems in merging home and work can be the gradual blurring of boundaries between private and public life. Here, privacy has been preserved by a dual-purpose entrance that helps to establish a buffer zone between the two. The front door leads into a wide entrance rather like an ante-room. At its rear is a sliding wall. With the wall positioned to the right, visitors can go up the staircase – a shot of warmth that demarcates the home. When the wall is moved the other way, the entrance becomes a reception area for the ground-floor office. The façade of the house remains from a 1980s renovation. The next phase of work will be to restore it to something more like the original.

OPPOSITE The mezzanine level in the extension houses a library and sitting area.

ABOVE The addition of a pristine kitchen with highly reflective surfaces brings modernity to the old house.

OVERLEAF (left) The kitchen opens into the new dining area. The mezzanine level above gives a sense of openness and height, while the bridge linking the old and new structures is treated as a service core, housing a cloakroom and storage space.

OVERLEAF (right) Light pours into the dining area through the huge glass doors.

A building that once housed artisans' workshops has been converted to provide a studio and home for an artist, while retaining the austere working character of the original

At street level, industrial doors open to provide access to the studio.

The original stone stairs have been retained and the back window now looks into the glass extension.

Before

The glazed dining area mediates between kitchen and terrace.

A nest-like sleeping platform is tucked into the apex of the roof.

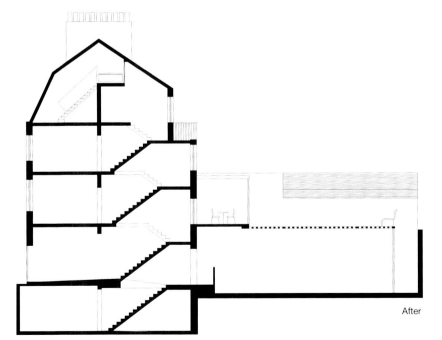

After

PREVIOUS PAGE The new shop front is divided in two. The front door leads into a wide hallway with an entrance to the studio on the right. Next to the front door, the glazed façade opens so that large paintings can be brought out through the office from the studio at the rear.

RIGHT The terrace on top of the studio functions as a continuation of the living floor, with the glass extension blurring the boundaries between indoors and out. The extension has an industrial glazing system that folds away, turning the area into a wall-less room.

OPPOSITE The ground floor was excavated so the studio could accommodate the artist's large canvases. It receives natural light via the pavement lights in the ceiling and a small courtyard at the rear.

Although it looks and functions much like a standard terraced town house, this five-storey, nineteenth-century house in the Brick Lane neighbourhood of London's East End was in fact built as a tenement, to house artisans' workshops. In remodelling the house for artist Chris Offili, architects David Adjaye and William Russell have played on the building's austere working character, translating the independent but inter-connected strands of work and home life into a series of narratives that occupy different levels of the house.

Offili's office and studio occupy the ground floor and basement. The work area extends all the way from the shop front to a narrow courtyard at the rear, jammed up against the party wall. The studio itself, which replaces old sheds built over what might once have been a backyard, is a contemporary reworking of an artist's atelier. In order to gain enough height so that large canvases can be hung and comfortably viewed, the ground has been excavated. At the entrance to the studio, a gallery overlooks the work space. This helps to create a physical and a psychological buffer between visitors and the intensely private territory of the artist's studio. The tough industrial treatment of the work space has been amplified by the concrete ceiling with its glass pavement lights and dramatic cross made of fluorescent tubes.

Above this, the living quarters occupy a sequence of spaces on the first floor. They run from the sitting room at the front, through the galley kitchen to a glazed box-like extension. This opens onto a terrace over the studio and helps to dissolve the boundaries between indoors and out. The terrace has the formality of an open-air living room, providing somewhere to enjoy unexpected views of surrounding buildings that include the mighty spire of Hawksmoor's Christ Church as well as the back elevations of Spitalfield's taciturn red-brick terraces.

The unusually substantial stone staircase, presumably designed to provide good access to the workshops, takes up as much as a third of the floor plate. Planning regulations governing combined live/work accommodation required its retention as a fire lobby. The architects have designed certain pieces of furniture for the landings – a seat and a telephone table – that help activate the circulation space.

On the top floor, the treatment of the master bedroom is as playful and unexpected as the entrance to the studio. The bed has been elevated to a platform at attic level so that it hangs, suspended, like a crow's nest, while the floor area below, lined with storage cupboards (one concealing a lavatory) has been left free of furniture. This manipulation of the space is characteristic of the way Adjaye and Russell work, making unexpected manoeuvres and connections that help us experience something as familiar as the terraced house in a completely unfamiliar way.

OPPOSITE **What was previously a back window now gives an unexpected view into the new glass extension.**

TOP **The passage creates a long view from the front of the house through the galley kitchen to the terrace at the back.**

ABOVE **The sitting room at the front is one of the few relatively conventional rooms remaining in the house.**

RIGHT In the master bedroom on the top floor, the floor space is left practically empty, while the bed is neatly inserted on a platform suspended in the pitch of the roof.

OPPOSITE (above and below) The self-contained sleeping area is designed to be a retreat, isolated from the activity of the house and with nothing to impinge but views of the sky.

In a low-budget conversion providing studio and family accommodation for an artist, the use of industrial components and materials reflects the working texture of the district

The lawn has been raised to first-floor level, on top of the studio roof. An external staircase leads to the children's bedroom above.

The new industrial staircase is in keeping with the open plan of the renovation.

Ground and first floors

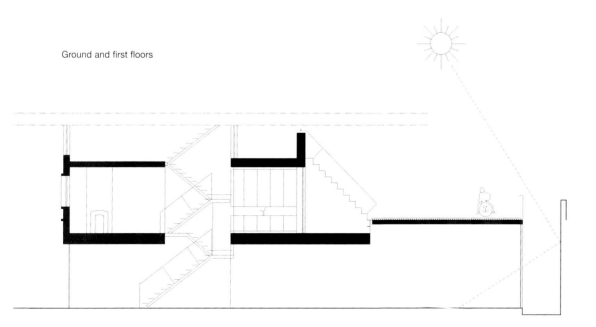

PREVIOUS PAGE In the renovation, emphasis has been given to outside as well as inside space, with stairs linking the terrace on the first floor to a balcony outside the children's bedroom.

ABOVE The kitchen extension at the rear has large windows opening onto the terrace. The greens and yellows of the cupboards echo the vivid green of the lawn planted in a thin layer of a special soil on the roof of the studio.

OPPOSITE The wall at the front of the living room is lined in plywood that may one day be used as a painting surface.

Fire escapes criss-crossing the backs of buildings are a familiar presence in many inner-city areas. In this conversion of a terraced house, skeletal fire-escape-like metal stairs are a leitmotif both indoors and out.

One of the key concerns of the owners in commissioning architect Trevor Horne to convert a derelict terraced house in an intensely urban district of central London into a family home, was to provide outdoor spaces for the children to play. The result is that, instead of a ground-level garden, a slab of green lawn now hovers rather surreally outside the first-floor kitchen window. External stairs connect this to a balcony outside the children's bedroom on the second floor, turning the exterior of the house into something resembling a giant climbing frame.

When the house was acquired, its chequered past as home, shop and, latterly, workshops had left it in a derelict condition. In the renovation, the ground floor still accommodates a shop at the front and behind this, in a new extension in the backyard, the artist's painting studio. Behind the studio, a small courtyard provides light, ventilation and a place outdoors for canvases to dry. The first floor has been enlarged by the extension housing the kitchen.

The most radical internal element of the renovation is the metal staircase that links the work quarters to the home above. Chosen, like the external staircase, to echo neighbouring fire escapes, its openness provides unexpected glimpses from the ground floor of life in the open-plan first-floor living room. It also functions as a light well, helping to bring daylight into the middle of the deep, enclosed, ground floor.

While the elementary materials and generic fittings used were necessitated by the tight budget, they are also very much a part of the project's blunt, understated aesthetic, where spatial organisation takes priority over expensive finishes.

A grid of large windows transforms a maisonette, shifting the emphasis from the front of the house to the garden at the back

The raised garden on a level with the ground floor provides long green views.

On the ground floor, one long room now overlooks the garden.

At basement level, the kitchen window opens onto a small courtyard.

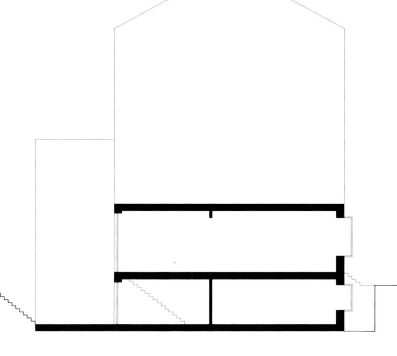

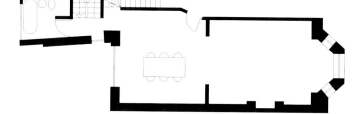

Ground floor

PAGE 43 **Massive windows give fresh impact to the back of the house, whose different levels are reflected in the design of the garden.**

OPPOSITE **Two rooms have been turned into one long living room. A passage leads to an earlier extension with a bathroom at ground-floor level and a turret-like bedroom above this.**

LEFT **At the back of the basement, wide floorboards visually extend the kitchen, which is divided from the room at the front by a bathroom and storage area.**

With the exception of the few estates planned around extensive communal back gardens, London's white stucco terraces tend to be all front. While their street façades are decorously uniform, the rear elevations are very often a tired hotchpotch of different-sized windows and piecemeal extensions held in place by a corset of pipework.

In a renovation of a basement and ground-floor maisonette for art dealer Thomas Dane, architect Thomas Croft reversed the original orientation, reordering the interior so that the emphasis is directed towards the garden. In the open-plan ground-floor living room and basement kitchen, the conventional rear windows have been replaced with massive rectangular plate-glass wood-framed windows that overlook the garden. Two other new windows belong to a bathroom and bedroom in an earlier extension. From the outside, especially at night when they glow, the immense windows bring a sense of order, at least to the lower part of the rear elevation.

Despite the idiosyncrasies typical of such garden elevations, London's planners are fairly strict. Here, the comparatively extreme alteration to the fenestration of the garden façade was allowed because it is hardly overlooked.

A conventional town house is
reconstructed to create an interior defined by spatial purity

The basement kitchen projects into the garden with a terrace at ground-floor level.

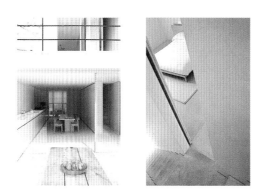

A dramatically narrow new staircase rises from ground to top floor with a landing at first-floor level.

The sense of calm and continuity throughout the house is enhanced by the limited palette of materials. Stone floors are used indoors and out.

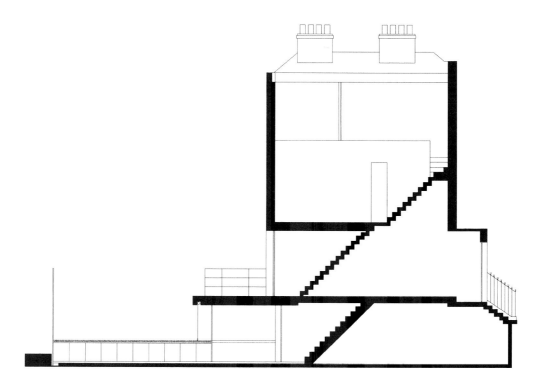

PAGE 47 **Conventional stairs were replaced by a dramatically narrow single flight illuminated by a skylight.**

PREVIOUS PAGES In the basement, the continuation of the kitchen counter through the glass wall helps create the illusion that the outdoor space is a mirror image of the interior space.

ABOVE The first-floor living room extends onto a terrace overlooking the garden.

One of the surprising aspects of even fairly modest town houses is their potential to evolve and be altered. Considering that such houses have been in existence as a basic architectural format for a couple of hundred years, they have proved a remarkably durable and adaptable container for domestic life.

Conservation regulations have ensured that most of London's acres of white stucco squares, terraces and crescents look similar from the outside, but their interiors are often another matter. In this house, remodelled by architect John Pawson for his own family, the existing plan has been rationalised to meet the needs of two adults and two children and dramatically manipulated to make an architectural statement that has little in common with the vision of its original builders.

The semi-detached house is relatively small – in all, little over 150 sq. m. (1600 sq. ft.) spread over four floors – yet its location gives it a sense of expansiveness. In an inversion of the usual design of London squares, here the houses back onto extensive communal gardens, giving a sense of space and long green vistas that are unusual in the city.

In terms of organisation, the house follows a similar pattern to that of many of its neighbours. The kitchen, the core of family life, is in the basement and extends into the garden. On the ground floor, the sitting room opens onto a terrace over the kitchen extension, while upstairs, the first floor is reserved for the parents and the children sleep on the top floor.

The staircase is the one element that has been constantly on the move throughout the history of the town house, driven either by the desire for effect or in order for it to take up as little

floor space as possible. Here the repositioning aims for both. In place of the original wooden stairs, a dramatic stone staircase now rises between sheer white walls from the back of the ground floor to the top of the house, with a second floor linking ground floor and basement. Height and compression give the new stairs a physical charge. This is enhanced by the cascade of light from a long narrow slit of skylight. The restructuring has also helped rationalise the plan, getting maximum use from each floor's 4m. (13ft.) width.

As well as making the surroundings – long views of sky and trees – a part of the interior experience, Pawson frames the physical connection between indoors and out in unexpected ways. In the basement, the kitchen is reduced to a single long stone counter that continues right through the rear glass wall to the end of the garden, seeming to dissolve the barrier between the inside and outside. On the top floor, a skylight opens electrically so you can shower in the open air.

While so-called minimalism has mushroomed into a full-blown style, the reductive purity of Pawson's architecture is a reminder that minimalism is about much more than a few coats of white paint and a lack of clutter, as it is often portrayed. Yet despite its rigour and formality, this house is not just a giant inhabited sculpture. It is first and foremost a home, its sparse interior conceived as a backdrop to family life that provides clarity and tranquillity – luxurious counterpoints to the cacophonous ebb and flow of urban existence.

ABOVE LEFT AND RIGHT The bedroom is at the back on the first floor, overlooking the garden and the bathroom is next door. The bath is a long stone trough running the width of the room, its massiveness reminiscent of ancient or religious washing places.

A conventional semi-detached family house
has been remodelled to make an open-plan home for a couple

Almost the only visible change to the exterior is the glass panel replacing the solid gable end.

Conventional stairs have been replaced by an open industrial metal staircase.

Screens are used to create privacy.

Before

After

From the outside of this pebble-dashed Tudorbethan Metroland semi-detached house in West London, where streets straggle from urban to suburban, there is little to suggest supersonic gentrification. Only the most observant might notice the extremely heavy-duty, rusting metal front door that came from a prison, or the triangular pane of glass that replaces the usual half-timbered panel in the gable end.

Inside is another matter. Even now, almost a decade after the conversion, when such transformations have become more usual, you still have a sense of amazement at the disjuncture between the exterior and the interior worlds.

In French architect Jeff Delsalle's elegant conversion for art director Yvonne Sporre, little more than the shell of the original house was retained. Instead, a conventional web of living rooms and four bedrooms has been replaced by two open-plan floors, one for living and one for sleeping.

On the ground floor, now open from front to back, the ceiling has been raised from 3m. (9ft.) to 3.5m. (11ft.), giving an unexpected sense of openness. This is enhanced by the skeletal metal staircase linking the two floors, and the large bathroom at landing level.

In the original house, the kitchen and bathroom would have been small, self-contained and strictly utilitarian. Now, not only is the kitchen a generous part of the living space and a place for eating as well as cooking, but the bathroom has grown to the same size. More than simply somewhere for bathing, it functions as a kind of sanctuary within the open-plan home and also as a dressing room and service room containing laundry equipment.

Maybe the most unexpected part of the transformation is the upper floor, which has been turned into a lofty room open to the pitch of the roof. Part of the attic has been retained as a small guest room and has a domed skylight. Reached by wall rungs, this room is known as 'the submarine'.

This is a conversion that has stood up remarkably well to the test of time and the unexpected mix of natural materials and industrial fittings has managed to avoid the trap of the over-designed. Sporre says that if she were redoing the project now, the only modifications she would consider would be a bedroom offering more privacy and a separate cloakroom on the ground floor.

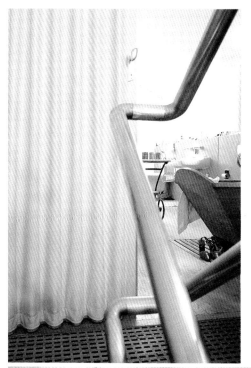

PAGE 53
A skeletal industrial staircase contributes to the new sense of openness in the living area.

OPPOSITE **Raising the ceiling of the ground floor has given a scale quite unexpected in a house of this sort.**

TOP AND ABOVE **The large bathroom is screened by a folding door made for hospital use. The room's furnishings reflect its role more as private sitting room than conventionally utilitarian wash place. A storage wall houses clothes and laundry.**

OVERLEAF **The sleeping floor is also one open space. Instead of there being a bedroom, the corner containing the Indian bed can be screened off. Wall rungs lead to 'the submarine' in the remaining section of attic.**

Canal Street, New York.

Industrial/Commercial

photo: Fred W. McDarrah

Over the past half century or so, the shift to living in former industrial and commercial buildings has helped precipitate a new way of urban living and also a new urban domestic typology. As well as reshaping the maps of cities, so-called loft-living has been enormously influential on our perception of urban life. From downtown Manhattan or Los Angeles, to London's East End and Docklands or Sydney's waterfront, the texture of inner-city life has changed, as whole districts that were once occupied by workshops, sweatshops, warehouses and manufacturing are now colonised for residential use and spiced with industrial-scaled art galleries, bars and restaurants.

The extent to which the loft has been embraced is reflected in the fact that now, not only do we convert pretty much any building into a so-called 'loft' but, more perversely still, we build new 'lofts' for the well-off which masquerade as warehousing or manufacturing buildings for industries that have long since vacated the city centre, if not the planet. In *Loft Living*, a critical study of the loft market, Sharon Zukin explores how an 'untested and unlikely sort of housing space – a loft – becomes a hot commodity' and how developers have capitalised on this new housing option.

Fifty years since the beginning of the loft movement, how we see and inhabit the loft, and the whole consumable lifestyle option (as it has become), has moved a long way. In *Architecture Must Burn*, American architect and critic Aaron Betsky sees the loft's enduring appeal as lying in the fact that it offers the

ABOVE Factory Party, 31 August 1963. In a midtown industrial building, Andy Warhol's first Factory, with its reflective silver interior, helped make the loft glamorous and happening.

possibility of *ad hoc* accommodation removed from the strictures of architecture in a way that reflects the fluidity of today's lives. According to Betsky, urban nomads 'want fluid and open spaces where they can work, live, play and then leave. These bare volumes have few characteristics; they are boxes whose shapes are completely contingent on the site, local ordinances and financing arrangements . . . They are the idealized space of modernism without its pure form.' For others, the appeal of open space has paled into unstructured sprawl. In a recent article in American *House & Garden* that proposes a return to the structured habitation, David Colman railed, 'What do you see in lofts that I don't? . . . I see nothing. No walls, no rooms, no direction, no flow – nothing but ghastly open space! What are you going to do with all of it? . . . Put up a few walls so you'll have a little privacy?'

In the beginning, the term 'loft' was used to describe the relatively large open space on each floor of a multi-storey industrial building or warehouse. The design was made as simple and open as possible: lines of columns holding up the ceilings to allow flexible floor space, large windows for maximum illumination, industrial materials and a paucity of decoration to keep costs as low as possible. Artists liked them because they offered raw, open and, above all, cheap space – and since then, others have followed.

Since the first lofts, the process of recycling decommissioned commercial buildings has been applied to more or less any building not originally intended for residential use, whether an office tower, or an institution such as a hospital or school. This trend reflects changing urban usage as manufacturing gives way to service industries, and civic buildings and the public sector are dismantled by privatisation. In this chapter, the examples given are not all lofts in the original sense of the term. Instead, the projects have been chosen to highlight different aspects of what has become a more universal process of recycling former non-residential buildings to make living spaces.

Originally, the habitation of industrial buildings was an American phenomenon, and New York City has been both the harbinger of and model for loft-living. In the 1940s and 1950s it was a radical, even politicised housing option pioneered by the Abstract Expressionist generation of artists, performers and photographers who required cheap space for living and working. SoHo's cast-iron buildings were still occupied by light industry, wholesalers and sweatshops. By day, the districts rumbled with deliveries, while at night, the industrial hulks stood as empty and dark as ships in mothballs. In the beginning, 'lofts' were neither chic nor comfortable, and were mostly considerably closer to the idea of a factory than to a home in the usual middle-class sense of the word.

A defining characteristic of first-generation lofts, if not of more recent incarnations, was the merger of work and living, making the home a place of production as well as of habitation. As Zukin has observed, 'Although homes are considered private space, the openness of a loft makes it a public space.'

Alterations to zoning laws have helped precipitate more widespread change. While the first lofts were commercial premises and habitation of them was often illegal, subsequent zoning-law changes have encouraged the merger of living and working and of commercial and residential, in a way that may not be permitted in residential districts.

Early loft buildings offered rudimentary living conditions, a kind of Beat Generation version of domesticity. In *Loft Living*, Zukin quotes writer Calvin Tompkins' description of artist Robert Rauschenberg's loft in 1953: 'a big attic space with twenty-foot ceilings but no heat or running water . . . A hose and bucket in the backyard served as a basin, and he bathed at friends' apartments, sometimes surreptitiously, asking to use the bathroom and taking a lightning shower at the same time.' The landlord asked for fifteen dollars a month rent but Rauschenberg managed to get it down to ten.

Another iconic example that helped invent the mythology of the loft was Andy Warhol's Factory – in its various guises and locations. Warhol moved into the first Factory in 1963, on the fifth floor of a warehouse building – previously a hat factory – in the shadow of the Empire State Building. The 30 x 12m. (100 x 40ft.) room with metal columns, a concrete floor and crumbling brickwork provided the location for a perpetual amphetamine-driven happening and a twenty-four-hour cult campsite. According to Warhol's biographer, Victor Bokris, Warhol acolyte Billy Linich laboured for four months, slowly turning the dark crumbling room into a giant reflector 'where the walls and floors, the ceiling and pipes, even the chairs and bar stools, the pay phone, the bathroom, the toilet bowl and the flushing mechanism were silver'. Light bounced around as in a hall of mirrors. Warhol even adopted a silver wig to match the Factory. 'Silver was the future,' Warhol later wrote, '. . . it was spacey – the astronauts . . . and silver was also the past – the Silver Screen . . . And maybe more than anything else, silver was narcissism – mirrors were backed with silver'. It was here that Warhol shot films like *Empire State Building* and *Blow Job*, and also where he was shot by Valerie S.

In terms of conservation, the late artist Donald Judd's restrained refurbishment of a SoHo loft building has become an influential precedent for sympathetic restoration and a SoHo landmark. Judd bought 101 Spring Street in the Cast-Iron District in 1968. Built in the 1870s, it was originally used for cloth manufacture. Judd used the building both as a place to live and work, and to display art by himself and others. It is still used as a showcase for Judd's work and for that of his minimalist peers like Dan Flavin.

The five-storey corner building with two basements was built on a long and narrow lot only 7.5 x 22.5m. (25 x 75ft.) and includes a right-angle of glass. Judd retained the original open floor plan and the working character of the building, as well as many internal details, such as the patterned ceilings and exposed network of pipes and sprinkler system.

If artists displaced small manufacturers, wholesale operations, garment sweatshops and so forth, they, in turn, have long since been squeezed out of SoHo by market prices as artists' studios and galleries have been transformed into fashion boutiques and now restaurants, giant fashion chains and cosmetics companies who use the 'loft' and 'gallery' aesthetic to frame their wares. In the former sweatshops of SoHo there are shops selling a chic take on the industrial loft aesthetic – aluminium diner chairs, lampshades the size of lifebuoys, and so on – to wealthy inhabitants prepared to buy into a style that was originally makeshift and bricolage. On Mercer Street there is an expensive hotel styled as a gentrified take on loft-living. Here the baths are enclosed by screens so that they can be opened up to become part of the room. According to owner André Balazs, this idea was inspired by his early days as a loft-dweller, when the shower was behind a curtain in the kitchen. How pervasive the desire to live in a loft has become is illustrated by the residents that downtown now attracts. Ageing media mogul Rupert Murdoch based his new life with his new wife in a SoHo loft. According to American *House & Garden*, the shift southwards in Manhattan over the last decade has turned the 1007 zip code of southern TriBeCa into the highest household income district in Manhattan, pushing the traditional wealth zone of the Upper East Side into second place.

It is ironic – but hardly unexpected – that while the appeal of the loft was once about freedom and about space without associations or boundaries, it has been swiftly codified in films and television

commercials and has come to represent a particular set of values or lifestyle. Free-living has long since been replaced by free-spending. As Marcus Fields and Mark Irving wrote in *Lofts*, 'From being zones of feisty individualism, lofts became about being rich, marketed as the places in which "movers and shakers" planned their next career spectacular.'

If the character and culture of so-called 'loft-living' has changed dramatically during the last couple of decades, so, too, has the way the 'raw space' of former industrial and commercial buildings is treated. In early lofts, living conditions were often rough in the extreme, but more recently lofts have become a playground and showcase for architects and designers.

The plan of the conventional house long ago came to enshrine conventional values of family and comfort, while much of the appeal of the open space of commercial buildings was that it seemed diametrically opposed to what some had come to see as the bondage of bourgeois domesticity. The empty industrial shell – in its most standard form, an open rectangle banded by windows at either end – literally presented a *tabula rasa*, a seedbed for alternative lifestyles, a space for new cultural identities to take root.

The habitation of commercial spaces might seem to undermine conventional ideas of domesticity and to present diametrically opposed problems to the conventional house or apartment, in terms of finding ways to subdivide rather than open up space, erect rather than dismantle walls. But the quest for airy, light,

open space in a former factory or office block is much the same as the quest that drives change in the suburban house or the town house.

Yet if the loft started out as a raw living space, spontaneously kitted out to meet *ad hoc* living requirements, how the characteristic rectangular space is treated has evolved considerably in the past thirty or forty years. The first lofts had few divisions: the only segregated areas were for private functions such as the lavatory, bathing and sometimes sleeping. In the beginning, the open plan of the loft celebrated space and was presumed to encapsulate flexibility. Since then, though, the limitations to openness have become apparent to many. As architect Zaha Hadid observes, 'the loft turned out to be nothing more than a closed plan with no doors in it'.

Increasingly, the spatial planning of today's lofts, in line with other domestic interiors, tends to be about creating more hybrid and flexible living spaces that reflect our conflicting needs and desires for open space and privacy, the personal and the shared, the social and the territorial, freedom and enclosure. This is reflected in a tendency to modulate rather than divide the space.

In the Wooster Street loft (pages 68–73), the 450 sq. m. (5000 sq. ft.) space is organised with a minimum of walls and doors. Instead, the different zones flow together and subtler devices are used to differentiate living from sleeping, public from private spaces. The most dramatic intervention is a wavy wall of semi-transparent glass which wraps around the master suite, more like a veil than a conventional wall. Devices like curtains, which can be closed around the interior of the bedroom, mean that more intimate spaces can be created within the larger spaces – and changed at will. This recalls something of the way textiles were used to modulate space in medieval homes.

How space is organised also reflects the shifting importance placed on certain activities and the boundaries between what we consider private and public. In the contemporary loft, certain configurations that reflect more general shifts in habitation, such as the open kitchen/eating area, are more or less universal. Sleeping and bathing tend to be separated from the public areas, although with increasing openness and changing views of sexuality, privacy is less important and, as in the Wooster Street loft, divisions are sometimes deliberately ambiguous.

One stratum of the city that can sometimes offer extraordinary and unexpected potential for development is the roof space, used not in the way that attics in houses are converted, but as a way to occupy the no-man's land often to be found on top of commercial and industrial buildings. In the Crépain

duplex (pages 94-7), the living quarters are contained in a glazed box added on top of the original warehouse building, making possible height, lightness and airiness and providing a link between indoors and outdoors that could not have been accommodated in the original structure.

In the Manhattan apartment (pages 90-93), New-York-based architects Lot/ek have tapped into the eccentric and clandestine, even lawless, territory of the roofscape memorably captured in Jim Jarmuseh's film *Ghost Dog*, where the Samurai dreamer exists in his own secret rooftop world shared by pigeons and an unbreakable code of honour. Lot/ek's bizarre assemblage of industrial flotsam far removed from the regulated, Cartesian logic of the city below, would surely never have been permitted at ground level in the centre of Manhattan.

Perhaps the attraction of the roof level is its sense of slight unreality, of infinite space within but slightly removed from the urban pressure cooker. Architect Bernard Tschumi proposed a programme of domestic rooftop development as 'a reaction against the dream of suburbia, rather than abandoning the city and recreating an artificial urban existence outside it'. His proposal for erecting luminous glasshouses in the sky on top of buildings 'addresses the city by existing both within it and above it'.

While the open plan of a commercial space may appear to offer freedom, there may be practical constraints – usually to do with the positioning of the windows and penetration of light – that dictate how a space is organised. The ideal loft may have high ceilings and substantial glazing, but in many industrial buildings developers scrimped and saved by using comparatively cramped ceiling heights.

Thus a common problem in long, low lofts, where windows are confined to either end, is that the area in the middle can be uninvitingly gloomy. Equally, it makes it difficult to introduce room divisions without blocking what light is available. For this reason, glass and other transparent materials are often used in lofts to create internal walls.

In a Manhattan loft (pages 78–83), two floors with comparatively low ceilings have been combined by cutting away a part of the floor to make a dramatic double-height living space. In addition, the end wall has been punched out and replaced with industrial glazing, giving an atelier-like appearance. The scale and proportions of this new space provide a focus for what would otherwise be a comparatively ordinary industrial space, showing how volume can be more important than square footage. In the house in a former industrial mews building designed by the young British practice Caruso St John, (pages 74–7), part of the upper storey has been removed to allow light into the rear of the building, lifting what would otherwise be a gloomily internalised space. Besides lighting, heating and acoustics can also present considerable problems in large, open spaces.

In the Parr loft in TriBeCa (opposite), the advantages of a top-floor position have been dramatically exploited by punching a row of windows in the blank side wall so the space now has spectacular views over the Hudson towards the Statue of Liberty. Yet this loft's most recent reincarnation illustrates another direction in loft-living, the so-called loft apartment. The long studio space at the front has subsequently been divided up to turn the whole floor plan into something more like a magnified version of a conventional apartment, with a series of rooms divided by a wide spinal corridor. The very openness that was once considered liberating is seen to have constraints of its own. Is it not deliciously perverse that we now install walls, doors, fireplaces and even corridors, those emblems of bourgeois living, in former industrial buildings?

While it is not unusual to find homes in former factories transmuted by decoration into ersatz suburban or country homes, or even into palazzo-esque fantasies, the habitation of former industrial buildings has had a massive influence on how we style our domestic environment. The high-tech movement had its roots in proto-Modernism going back as far as the industrially made Crystal Palace and continuing through such buildings as the Eames house or the Centre Pompidou. But it is really the loft that has helped domesticate and popularise this industrial aesthetic. After all, borrowing elements intended for industrial use to serve domestic purposes makes sense when you are living in an industrial building.

Kron and Slesin's influential source book *High-Tech,* published in the United States in 1978, celebrated the use of industrial artefacts in the domestic landscape, exploring the residential potential in everything from greenhouse glazing and scaffolding systems to factory-scaled space heaters, industrial cooking ranges, and so forth. It became the handbook for loft-dwelling.

Yet some of today's more adventurous practitioners work in unexpected ways. Lot/ek have developed a contemporary design language by finding unexpected uses for old industrial components. Rather than organised recycling, where used artefacts are returned to a material state, the Lot/ek approach is closer to the process of creative re-use in developing countries, where decorated sandals may be fashioned from old tyre rubber or whole peasant villages can be constructed from the debris of wealthier societies.

Caruso St John takes another approach to the existing urban landscape, looking for ways to alter our perception of the ordinary rather than eradicate what exists. In the house designed by them (pages 74–7),

the conventional façade has been replaced by a wall of opaque glass that lets light into the rather dark interior and also provides a high degree of insulation. Inside, a small budget forced such solutions as retaining walls scarred with the marks of old pipes and paper, and using bare plasterboard patterned with the lines of the tape that holds the sheets together. Such an aesthetic celebrates history and memory in a way that is ruled out in the gleaming surfaces of high-tech.

But this aesthetic is also very different from the other, depressing, side of industrial nostalgia that pervades many former industrial and commercial developments. In these, now that sweat and labour and low wages have long been forgotten, old hoists, freight elevators and other discarded industrial artefacts are romanticised as 'features' much as horse brasses and dried hops decorate pubs in country suburbs where lawnmowers and strimmers have taken over from tractors and combine harvesters.

Taking advantage of its position adjacent to a parking lot, the top floor of an industrial building has been transformed by punching a row of windows in the brick wall. The result is spectacular views from the loft apartment and a light-filled interior.

In a Manhattan loft, open-plan living has evolved into a sequence of zones differentiated by materials

The living area is open plan, structured by a line of columns and the positioning of the kitchen and furniture.

A translucent glass wall separates the private areas from the living quarters.

The bathroom is the centre of the master suite, with the bedroom on one side and the library on the other.

Rich, textural materials give different areas their individual character.

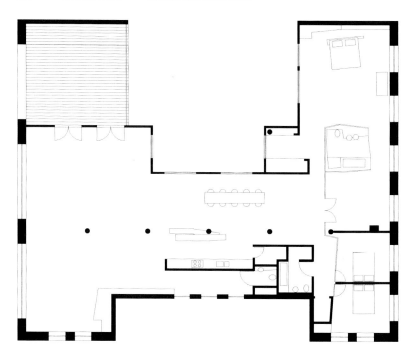

Translucent glass
and shimmering
metal bring an
unexpected
lightness to the
industrial interior.

PREVIOUS PAGES
The open-plan living
area with half-moon
windows and a line
of columns retains
something of the
industrial character
of the original
building.

LEFT The master
suite is enclosed by
a long, wavy wall of
translucent glass.

RIGHT The bedroom
area is warmed by
the use of luxurious
materials. The walls,
for example, are
lined with walnut.

Manhattan-based Dutch architect Winka Dubbeldam's treatment of this large and luxuriously budgeted loft conversion for an art collector in a substantial nineteenth-century industrial building in downtown Manhattan is very much in line with current experiments in loft living. Instead of juxtaposing an open-plan living area with conventional self-contained bedrooms, the need for personal and communal space is accommodated in different 'zones' that flow into one another, emphasising spatial continuity and reflecting the fluidity of contemporary living patterns.

The defining element in structuring the 450 sq. m. (5000 sq. ft.) floor area is a long glass wall. Instead of being an inert and opaque division, it is a translucent wrapper whose wobbly, bulging form emphasises the blurring of boundaries between private and public areas. On one side, it folds around the expansive master suite, screening it, if not completely separating it, from the living quarters. On the other side is the L-shaped open-plan living area.

Here, the first zone is devoted to kitchen and dining. Beyond that is the sitting area and beyond that is a terrace. The only part of the loft that is self-contained in any conventional sense of the word are the guest quarters.

Dubbeldam describes the homes she designs not as showcases for personalities, but as places for them to relax. In line with this, she has devoted a substantial area to the master suite. Here, bedroom, bathroom and library run together in an extravagantly large, sensual zone, differentiated from the living area by the use of luxurious materials and textures that help to create a sense of warmth and intimacy.

While bathing was once a strictly private activity carried out behind closed doors, this is no longer necessarily the case. Here it is integrated into home life – even eroticised – in unexpected ways. Dubbeldam describes the intense blue bathroom of this loft as a 'free-floating capsule', and uses it as a hinge around which spaces unfold. On one side it is open to the bedroom and on the other to the library. The sound of water can be heard in the living area and the blurred silhouettes of bathers are just visible through the semi-opaque glass wall.

The emphasis now placed on bathing acknowledges the fact that in our increasingly hectic lives, the bathroom can be much more than just a place for washing. Often it is somewhere to go to relax. The juxtaposition of bathroom, bedroom and library acknowledges the fact that bath, bed and books can be intimately connected, for bathroom and bedroom may be places where we have time – and are in the frame of mind – to read.

Materials define and characterise the loft's different spaces. The bathroom is treated as a deep purple-blue island. Its built-in bath, shower and counter, as well as its floor, are all finished in smooth plaster so that they meld into one giant, sculptural unit. The bedroom walls are lined in walnut and grey suede curtains are used to create a room within a room, recalling the way fabrics were sometimes used as screens before the advent of effective central heating.

A robust, low-budget conversion of
a small mews building plays on its industrial origins
and the poetics of the everyday

The original brick façade has been replaced by opaque insulated glass panels.

Part of the upper storey has been sliced away to bring light into the rear.

The staircase and kitchen, and bathroom above, are housed in an MDF box.

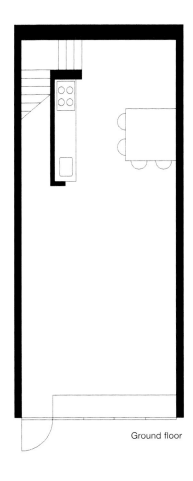

Ground floor

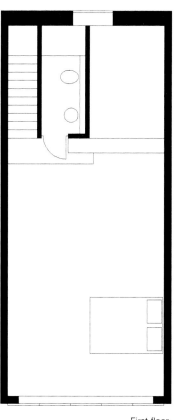

First floor

Architects Caruso St John, acclaimed for their design for the new Walsall Art Gallery in the West Midlands, cut their teeth during the recession of the early 1990s. These circumstances helped frame their dexterous approach to existing buildings. The low-budget conversion of a small building in an industrial yard in north London into Caruso's own home is a characteristically bold intervention that makes creative use of what exists. 'If you look hard enough, you usually find ways in which the structure lets you do what you have to do,' says Caruso.

Here, the most radical element is the treatment of the façade. The original brick was replaced by a screen of large glass panels, a sandwich of materials with similar insulating properties to those of the original wall. As well as maximising daylight and, according to conditions outside, bringing constant change to the interior, the translucent filter creates a sense of seclusion – a buffer to the activity of the yard.

Inside, the approach is equally uncompromising. The ground floor, which was first used as offices for the fledgling architectural practice, is a now a living space. If the effect of the almost opaque façade is a sense of internalisation, this feeling is balanced here by additional light filtering down where a slice of the upper storey has been removed to make an internal lightwell. Services and the staircase are installed in a box-like MDF core, with the kitchen on the ground floor and the bathroom above it, next to the bedroom.

A similar blunt approach governs the building's aesthetic. The walls have been left much as they were found in the derelict building. The patterns made by shards of old wallpaper and water stains read like a map of the building's past. In the new context they take on an unexpected beauty, just as the industrial fittings and everyday materials are used in a way that allows us to see the ordinary in a new light.

PREVIOUS PAGE **This view shows how the removal of part of the upper storey creates light and height.**

ABOVE **At ground-floor level the walls are left as rough brick and above this are lined with plasterboard.**

RIGHT **Sections of the translucent façade can be removed for ventilation.**

A duplex loft apartment is organised around a double-height living area, giving unexpected scale and light to a downtown industrial building

Two floors of an industrial building have been combined to make a modern loft.

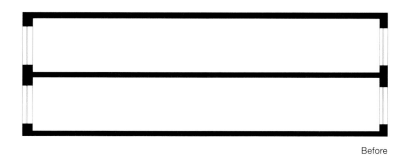

Before

Part of the upper floor has been removed to create a dramatically tall living area with a glazed wall replacing windows at the back.

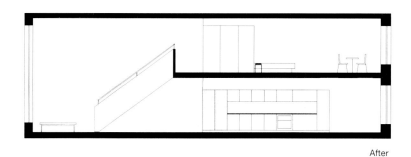

After

The wide gallery overlooking the living area provides access to the bedrooms.

Loft living is usually about life on the horizontal, but while some industrial buildings have good ceiling heights and generous windows, in others, commercial imperatives have forced ceilings down to almost oppressively low levels. The result can be conversions where, once you step away from the windows, you enter a gloomy interior no-man's land.

In this Manhattan loft in a former industrial building downtown to the west of SoHo, the owners bucked the problem of relatively low ceilings weighted down with a grid of projecting concrete beams, by incorporating two floors in one unit. Architects Fernlund and Logan linked the two storeys by cutting out a quarter of the upper floor, so making a double-height living space. They also replaced the original double row of three windows at the back with a massive aperture on the scale of a glazed wall.

Although conventional real-estate wisdom tends to be obsessed with the maximisation of living space above all else, and would probably regard such a dramatic reduction in floor area as lunacy, the height and light of this loft is what gives it a sense of focus and character. As you enter through the kitchen, the dramatic change in ceiling height brings a powerful sense of relief. The emphatic, rectangular grid of the new windows makes reference to the surrounding industrial buildings and also dramatically frames the gritty urban stage-set view. At night, it looks slightly unreal, almost like a video wall.

The volume of the living space, with its massive glazing and stairs positioned against one wall leading up to a gallery, recalls the tradition of the artist's atelier and such modern paradigms as the double-height apartment units in Le Corbusier's Unité d'Habitation in Marseilles.

Both upstairs and downstairs, the other rooms are organised in a large L-shape that wraps around the imposing living space. On the lower floor there is a studio for one of the owners who is a painter, and an office for the other, a film director. Upstairs, the gallery functions as a wide corridor, providing access to the bedrooms behind. In the guest room and the children's rooms, doors slide away so that these rooms can be either self-contained or opened up in different configurations.

Fernlund and Logan's approach plays with understatement, deliberately combining the coarse and the refined to give the building a textural history that bridges old and new. Existing industrial elements, such as the rough concrete columns and the network of concrete beams on the ceiling, contrast with the smooth texture of new walls and concrete floor. 'The clients wanted to retain some of the existing qualities,' says Logan. 'They chose a loft building because they wanted to live in a converted industrial space and we didn't want to lose this.'

PAGE 79 **The kitchen, located near the entrance, and the living room behind are differentiated by a dramatic change in ceiling height.**

PREVIOUS PAGES **The emphatic grid of the new window defines the living area and is echoed by the bookcases.**

OPPOSITE (above) **A wide gallery opens into the bedroom area and links the front and back of the building.**

OPPOSITE (below) **The internal bathroom between the master bedroom and the gallery has long slit windows on both sides to let in light from the adjacent areas.**

The conversion of a former canteen building exploits its green setting and generous scale

A new staircase links the ground-floor living area with the more intimate living quarters and bedrooms above.

The large kitchen is central to the living space. Here materials are mixed to create sensual richness.

Part of the first floor has been removed to make a double-height living area and mezzanine library.

PAGE 85 **The removal of part of the first floor makes a double-height sitting room downstairs and a more intimate sitting area and library overlooking it.**

PREVIOUS PAGES **The juxtaposition of wood, marble and stainless steel in the kitchen combines practicality and aesthetics.**

OPPOSITE **New industrial-scale glazing makes the most of the building's garden setting.**

RIGHT (above) **An open passage links the bedroom, dressing room and bathroom.**

RIGHT(below) **In the master bedroom Dordoni plays on the scale of the room with theatrical furniture.**

Although this former canteen building was part of a factory complex, there is little to indicate that this was the case. This has less to do with the actual buildings than with their unexpected setting in a large garden in the centre of Milan. Architect Rodolfo Dordoni, who converted part of the building for his own use, considers the relationship between indoors and outdoors to be pivotal. He describes the two-storey house flanked by a terrace as a 'loggia' and considers it as a covered part of a much larger composition.

Another impressive aspect is its scale. The building has been divided vertically into two units of 500sq. m. (5500sq. ft.) per floor, with ceiling heights of 3.5m. (11ft.). In its former life, the workers' *cantina* or refectory was on the ground floor and on the first floor were showers and dressing rooms. Dordoni removed the internal divisions but the main changes to the structure were the replacement of the relatively small windows by industrial-scale glazing, and the cutting out of part of the first floor to make a double-height living room.

Despite enjoying the luxury of space, Dordoni was clear from the outset that he did not want to feel as if he were living in a hotel or villa. As he was designing for a single inhabitant, he said he did not require more rooms and therefore they could be on a larger scale. The programme (three bedrooms and bathrooms, a kitchen and living room) is much what you would find in a conventional apartment, but luxuriously amplified.

In order of importance to his vision of a home, Dordoni places the kitchen first, followed by the bathroom: 'The kitchen is a place for sociability; the bathroom is more intimate space.' Next comes a big bedroom, followed by somewhere for friends to stay. In the kitchen, the mix of solid waxed mahogany, marble and stainless steel was chosen for texture and sensuality, which Dordoni considers to be an important part of the cooking experience.

Dordoni's furniture deliberately plays up to the scale, giving the interior a stage-like quality. One table is 4m. (13ft.) long. The unexpected mix of Modernist pieces and the combinations of materials give the home an idiosyncratic elegance.

If the process of domesticating our industrial and commercial past continues, business parks might some day be turned into loft parks. But the extraordinary thing about this loft is its green space, found here not in some suburban ribbon development, but in the centre of a city.

A Manhattan rooftop apartment has been created out of the debris of the industrial landscape

A cargo container has been recycled to make a high-level bedroom.

Part of the skin of the container has been removed to make space for a roof terrace.

The end wall of the container has been replaced by a pre-fabricated aluminium glazing system.

Inside, industrial recycling continues with old refrigerators used for storage.

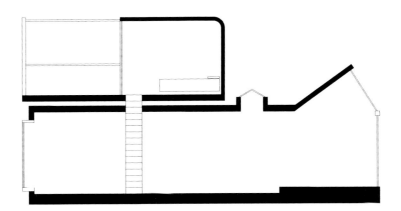

In a city as densely packed as Manhattan, sometimes the only room for expansion is upwards. Zeroing into the skyline, you find an unexpected jumble of buildings on top of buildings. As well as legitimate penthouses, elaborate roof gardens and conical water towers, all manner of maverick structures colonise the rooftops. Few though, are quite as deliciously incongruous as the yellow cargo container parked on top of a florid late nineteenth-century office building dressed up in Italianate ornamentation.

Loft living is all about reusing the building blocks of the industrial landscape for domestic purposes, but New York-based Italian architects Lot/ek have extended this definition by their approach to urban existence, an approach that they describe as 'recycling urban detritus into utilitarian facilities'.

Appropriately, the lower level of this unlikely penthouse designed for two photographers occupies a disused plant room. The living quarters are housed in a space that once contained the substantial machinery required to run an old-fashioned elevator. Essentially, this living area is one long space with windows at either end, and an alcove housing the kitchen and bathroom next to it.

Lot/ek resolved the need for extra space by deploying a cargo container on top of the plant room. Accessed by a metal ladder, the container has become a ready-made bedroom. It has also been bisected and part of its metal skin cut away to expose its skeletal structure. This now provides the framework for a roof terrace.

The imaginative recycling of industrial elements continues inside the penthouse. Refrigerators inserted in the wall serve as cupboards, while in the bedroom, reclaimed tool boxes are used for further storage. Whereas the high-tech movement was characterised by a hard-edged industrial aesthetic expressed through the use of prefabricated building kits and industrial components parts, Lot/ek go about it the other way round, trawling the massive reservoir of industrial waste to find cast-offs that they can recycle. The effect relies on an unexpected, even poetic, sense of transformation, an approach that is closer in spirit to the way a tin can or a car tyre is reused in developing countries than to the developed world's more formalised treatment of scrap as material to be pulped and then re-formed into something new.

A loft apartment combines the
top floor of a warehouse with a dramatic rooftop extension

The living quarters are housed in an extension on the roof of the warehouse.

The top floor of the original building retains its warehouse character, with cast-iron columns and vaulted ceiling.

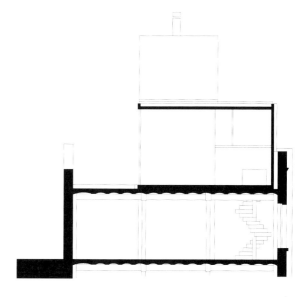

The extension has a glazed façade that opens onto the roof terrace.

The terrace takes advantage of the spectacular views. Outdoor furniture echoes the sculptural simplicity of the furniture indoors.

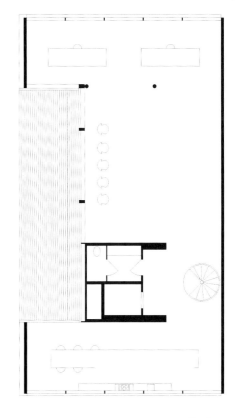

Top floor

This development by Flemish architect Jo Crépain in the centre of Antwerp is an unexpected take on that slightly meaningless loft-speak jargon 'live work'. The former coffee warehouse dating from c.1910 has been converted to house an architectural office for some forty staff on three floors, with Crépain's duplex loft apartment above. The original building retains the vaulted brickwork arches of the ceiling and its cast-iron pillars. The key alteration here was the replacement of an old industrial lift by a black-lacquered concrete shaft combining lift and stairwell. The apartment combines the upper storey of the original building and a dramatic rooftop addition, designed to take advantage of the light, the quietness of the aerial position and views that skim the skyline.

The brief for the loft apartment required living quarters for a couple, space for their art collection, a roof terrace, a master bedroom, a guest room and an atelier. The sleeping quarters and atelier are on the top floor of the original building, while the 4m. (13ft.) high extension above houses the living quarters. The two floors are linked by a sculptural spiral staircase sheathed in a metal cylinder.

The box-like extension is treated with rigorous simplicity, with a massive glazed wall that opens onto the terrace overlooking the river. The outer surface of the box is clad in aluminium while inside, the walls and ceiling are bare concrete. Wooden floors made from broad planks accentuate the sober character of the living space. The aluminium kitchen, dominated by a long counter that dissolves into an eating area, was designed by Crépain's team in collaboration with Maarten van Severen, the Belgian designer of elegant minimalist furniture. The counter is echoed by the strict geometry of the wall of books and by van Severen's long metal tables.

Crépain describes his approach as 'functionalist minimalist'. His earliest works go back to the 1970s, long before the recent wave of popularity turned minimalism into high-street currency. 'My house must be able to adapt to all my moods,' says Crépain. 'That is why an airy flexible spatial quality and a good combination of natural and artificial light are fundamental factors.'

PAGE 95 **The simplicity of the long counter/table, echoed by the row of lights, is in keeping with the sober character.**

OPPOSITE **The spiral staircase is contained in a sleek cylinder.**

ABOVE **A large part of the rooftop extension is given over to a roof terrace with a glazed façade linking it to the living area, so the whole space is like a gallery overlooking the city.**

LEFT **In the extension, columns and bare concrete walls are a modern interpretation of the original warehouse.**

A low-cost plywood installation makes
a work space habitable

The former factory complex has been converted to provide work spaces and living accommodation.

A new window transforms the internal space.

Rudimentary living quarters are contained in a 'crate' installed in the work space.

French artist Jérôme Mazerat describes his studio/home in a former factory building as a 'packing case'. The analogy refers to the crate-like two-storey plywood unit he has installed to provide low-cost living quarters and services in a work space.

The studio is to be found deep within the bowels of a building that was formerly owned by the SNCF, the French state-owned railway. It was originally lit only by a skylight. Mazerat put a large window in the back wall, revealing a gritty view over the railway lines. In front of this is his 'living unit'. On one side, next to the new window, the unit houses a compact office and seating area, and on the other, a rudimentary kitchen, behind which is the bathroom. The upper deck of the 'crate' is treated like a gallery, with two bedrooms overlooking the work space. Although decidedly basic, the raw plywood brings a sense of warmth to the industrial space and helps differentiate between living and work areas.

OPPOSITE Installed inside the studio, the plywood living unit has an entirely different character from the work space. On one side is a small office and sitting area.

ABOVE The lower level houses a tiny kitchen and, behind, the bathroom.

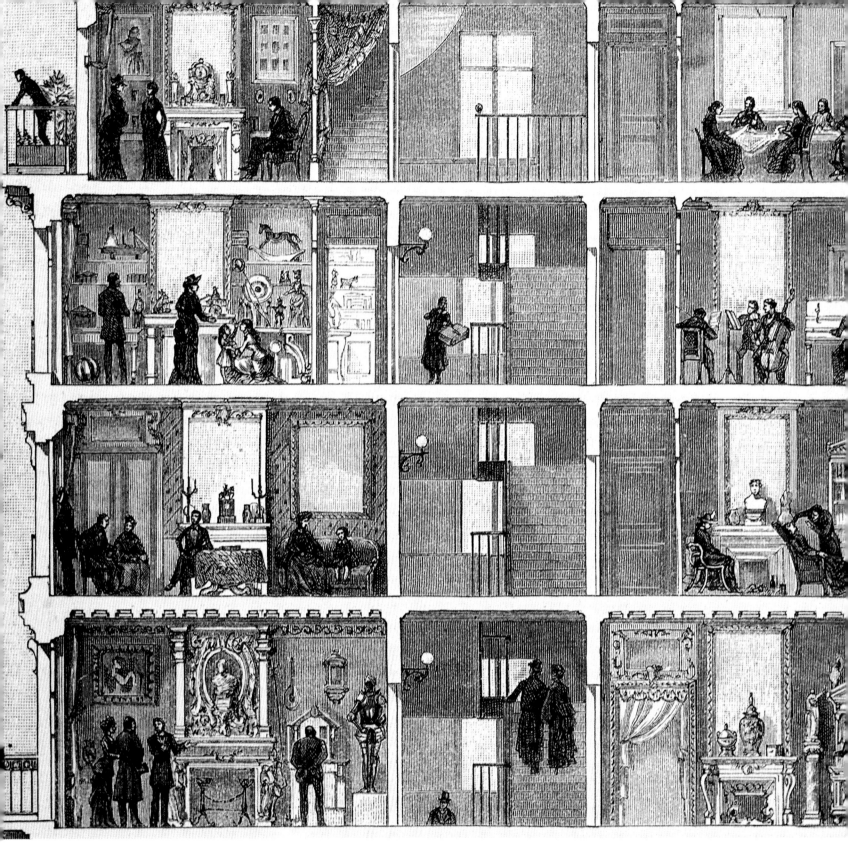

A high-rise apartment building, Paris, c.1880.

Apartment

Although there has been apartment-type housing in cities, from the time of ancient Rome with its tenements to the age of Dickens and the slums of London, it was the rapid expansion of industrialised cities in the nineteenth century that made the flat and the purpose-built apartment building increasingly common currency in the housing market. The apartment's early popularity owed much to two factors: it provided spatially compact housing in cities with rapidly increasing populations and it made it possible for the burgeoning industrial middle classes to buy into the urban explosion.

Today the term 'apartment' is very loose, and may simply mean a flat in a converted house. As with current trends in transforming town and suburban houses, the tendency in apartment conversion has been to break down the formal hierarchy of rooms and incorporate the area once given over to circulation and corridors into more flexible living spaces. In the past hundred or so years, the purpose-built apartment has emerged as a kind of consumer home product tailored to the housing needs of urban families at different social and income levels. This quest to design model apartments that provide a framework for basic human needs has generated progressive visions of how we can live that have more universal relevance.

Usually lacking either the scale of the loft or the possibility to separate activities by level that is characteristic of the house, the densely structured and served spaces of the apartment have been especially fruitful in propagating new ideas of how we can inhabit our living spaces. Pioneering modern architects used the model apartment as a domestic paradigm: model dwellings for the model modern family, and all sorts of spatial and functional arrangements that originated in experimental apartment design have filtered through to influence how we organise our living spaces.

Among the most influential Modern Movement apartments was the domestic cell designed by Le Corbusier for the Unité d'Habitation in Marseilles, 1949-52, which the architect hoped would become a prototype for low-cost housing. Drawing on ideas that had existed as early as his Citrohan housing units of the 1920s, the Unité apartment combined a double-height living room with a glazed wall on one side and a single-height bedroom zone on the other. The dual orientation maximised natural light and allowed for cross-ventilation. Reflecting the new domestic role of the woman in the servantless home, the kitchen was integrated into the living space. While the design rejected the formality of the bourgeois apartment, it made reference to other building forms, such as the purpose-built, nineteenth-century artist's atelier. The influence of Le Corbusier's apartment can still be seen in such recent housing projects as Jean Nouvel's Nemausus in Nîmes, where split-level apartments have dual orientation and a double- or triple-height living space.

If early Modernism was driven by an optimistic view of an ever-better society, in the post-war period that vision was slowly dismantled. And as utopian housing schemes degenerated into high-rise horror, a new spirit of social freedom and the increasing acceptance of a plurality of lifestyles emerged. Architects and designers began to explore approaches that allowed the user to take control, shaping and altering living spaces according to individual, unpredictable and changing needs.

LEFT AND RIGHT In the Unité d'Habitation, Marseilles, 1949-52, Le Corbusier developed the plan for a model apartment with a double-height glazed living space.

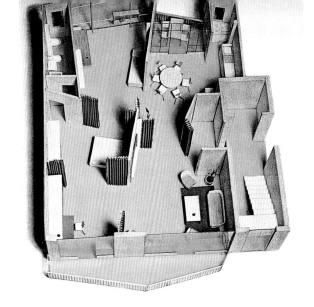

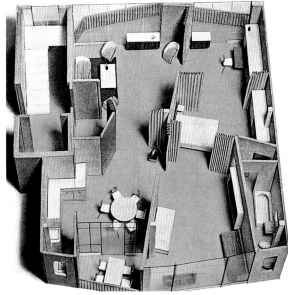

As the walls of the conventional apartment were removed, so the whole concept and function of the wall has been re-invented. Gio Ponti's 'Single Space Housing for Four People', published in *Domus* magazine in 1956, was described as a 'movable labyrinth'. Kitchen and bathroom and certain pieces of furniture were built into the perimeter walls, while the internal walls had folding movable panels that made it possible to isolate or connect different spaces.

Such ideas reveal the continual conflict – especially in the design of small apartments – between how to accommodate services, equipment and storage and how to retain a sense of unencumbered space. A recent design by Dante Donegani and Giovanni Lauda for a model living space, where services and storage are incorporated in heavily equipped 'thick walls', reflects current design directions. Here, the apartment first appears as a long, rectangular, empty white space. It can be transformed by a series of 'custom-made fully equipped boxes' that are pulled out of the walls. Some incorporate storage and others are actually habitable 'rooms', like the mini-gym, the office incorporating a desk unit, or the children's play area enclosed in a wigwam. As the designers have observed, 'love of empty space does not preclude a customer's pleasure'.

In the Paris apartment designed by François Roche (pages 114–19), the central wall dividing two living rooms becomes a multi-functional unit that provides all that is needed to activate the two spaces. On the kitchen side, the wall contains the services and storage, from cooking equipment to laundry and groceries. To avoid having to shuffle through cupboards to find what you want, everything is half-visible behind semi-opaque plastic doors.

LEFT **In a project entitled 'Single Space Housing for Four People', 1956, Gio Ponti breaks away from the cellular room plan to make a space that can be subdivided in different ways using folding screens instead of conventional walls.**

Another approach that is also influencing living design today explores ways to incorporate services and equipment in freestanding furniture-like elements. In the landmark exhibition 'Italy: The New Domestic Landscape', at New York's Museum of Modern Art in 1972, a number of designers proposed futuristic habitats where the architecture was seen as little more than a container and where services and equipment were incorporated in custom-designed furniture-like elements. Joe Colombo's Total Furnishing Units were four highly equipped mono-blocks: Kitchen, Cupboard, Bed and Privacy, and Bathroom. These autonomous units were suitable for any space and could be freely positioned, like furniture, to allow maximum freedom in a minimal living space. At the exhibition, the units were exhibited back to back, occupying an area of only 28sq. m. (31sq. yd.).

Although such futuristic habitats and integrated systems have yet to be adopted in other than a handful of custom-designed apartments, ways to inhabit space differently according to different needs and the idea of the convertible space have become more usual. In the 50sq. m. (60sq. yd) Halliday apartment (pages 112–13), one room is used for cooking and eating and the other for relaxing and sleeping. Each space is served by a custom-designed unit – one a single long kitchen counter and the other a box that has a seating alcove in its front, a dressing room inside and a bed on top. In a similarly sized Paris apartment (pages 120–21), the bed is also raised to mezzanine level, but the living space, instead of being opened out, is divided into two areas with distinctively different characters by a substantial storage wall with circulation space at either end.

Such ideas reveal the two-way flow of influence between loft and apartment, as we increasingly seek ways to create different living conditions to balance the contained and the open, the private and the shared, without returning to the old constrictions of the cellular room plan.

ABOVE **In this project for a model apartment by Dante Donegani and Giovanni Lauda, 1997, the blank, open, white living space is activated by boxes which pull out of the walls for different uses, and can be customised according to the owner's needs.**

Two apartments joined into one are designed so the outlook becomes part of the interior plan

Ground- and first-floor apartments overlooking the Seine have been turned into a duplex.

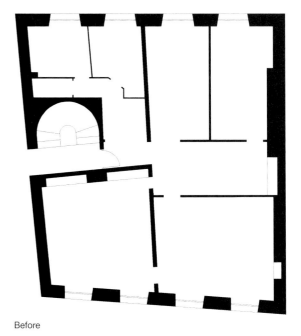

Before

New internal stairs link previously separate apartments.

A series of openings in one wall link peripheral rooms like the kitchen to the living area.

Further openings connect the library/dining area to the main room.

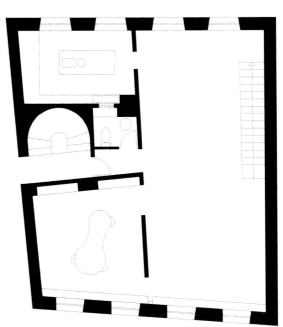

After

PREVIOUS PAGE **The spectacular view across to the Right Bank, at a point where the Seine is comparatively narrow, gives the apartment its defining character.**

RIGHT **Looking towards the back of the apartment clearly shows how the wall is used to structure the living space. The series of openings, subtly varying in width, link the open area to the ancillary rooms.**

PAGE 110 **The new staircase leading from the entrance arrives at the back of the first floor, so you take in the room before the view from the windows.**

PAGE 111 **Two openings in the wall link the library to the living area. The reflective surface of the giant peanut-shaped table by Ron Arad dominates the library.**

Surroundings can be part of the experience of a living space, a visual backdrop to everyday life that is just as tangible as the colour of the walls. In urban apartments, especially, what's on the outside can be as important as what's inside. This is certainly true of this Parisian apartment, but then its location is pretty remarkable.

The Ile de la Cité – the site of the original Gallic settlement that was to become Paris – is the boat-shaped island moored to the banks of the Seine by bridges. From this north-facing first floor of a relatively ordinary building, the Right Bank is laid out in a panorama. At night, roving searchlights from the *bateaux mouches* turn the living room into a magic lantern, with shadows of the wrought-iron window balustrades sweeping across walls and ceiling.

This apartment was designed for an art director by architect Philippe Boisselier, who had the unusual opportunity of returning to remodel and extend what he had previously renovated for the same owner. The first stage had been to convert a conventional five-room apartment into a more open living space, with one main room extending from front to back, making use of the light from either end. The second stage was to incorporate the flat below, turning the apartment into a duplex, with sleeping downstairs and living upstairs.

The layout is planned so that it does not give the game away at once. The entrance from the street leads directly to a staircase positioned so that you arrive at the back of the main room on the first floor. You then have to turn round and take in the whole space before getting sucked into the mesmerising view from the front windows.

The pivotal element structuring the main room is the long wall punctuated by a series of openings. This wall links the living space to the more functional elements that are set slightly backstage. Two openings give onto the library/dining area, positioned at the front of the apartment to take advantage of the view. Next comes the cloakroom, and at the back, the kitchen, partly enclosed so that it does not impinge on the main living space. From the entrance, the kitchen looks almost abstract, the dark grey stone of its island counter set against softer grey walls.

In a two-room apartment, living
functions are accommodated in two discrete units

Kitchen services are contained in a freestanding counter and storage unit in the entance room.

A freestanding box accommodates seating in front, a dressing room at the back, and a bed above.

The ceiling height allows for a bed on top of the box.

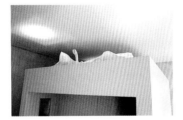

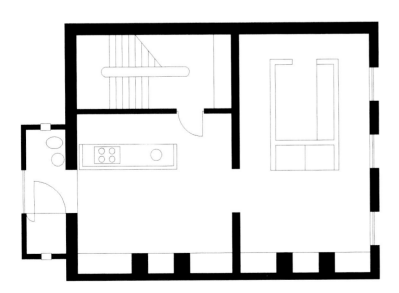

How much can go on in a small space without losing a sense of openness, order and visual calm? In converting a single 50sq. m. (60sq. yd.) floor of a Victorian house for his own use, Iain Halliday, partner with Sydney architects Burley Katon Halliday, was concerned to strip away period ornament yet retain the integrity and proportions of what are still recognisably Victorian rooms. Instead of dividing the space, the essentials for living are accommodated in two freestanding units installed in the rooms rather like pieces of furniture. In addition, one wall is entirely devoted to storage.

In the entrance room, the kitchen is reduced to a unit comprising a single counter with a dwarf wall to conceal any mess from view. In the living room, apart from a lone chair, the functions of sleeping, entertaining and dressing are all contained in a large open-sided box rather like a child's play house. The front of the box houses a sofa (what Halliday describes as 'the most cumbersome but necessary piece of furniture in a small apartment'). Behind that is a dressing room and on top, taking advantage of the 3.1m. (10ft.) ceiling height, is the bed. A shower room and toilet are in an enclosed balcony at the back of the apartment.

LEFT In the two-room apartment, period details have been stripped away but the original proportions of the rooms retained. Instead of cluttering the space with furniture, seating and bed are contained in the box unit.

In this robust conversion of a conventional apartment, kitchen and bathroom are reconfigured as transparent elements at the heart of the home

The apartment occupies the upper two floors of a nineteenth-century building.

Two rooms interconnect, with the library on one side and the kitchen on the other.

In the kitchen, equipment and services are half-concealed in a wall of transparent cupboards.

The bathroom in the master bedroom is installed in a transparent cubicle.

PAGE 115 **The kitchen wall is a multi-purpose service facility incorporating laundry, storage and television. Different sections can be opened up as needed.**

PREVIOUS PAGES The design of the kitchen has been treated with utilitar ian directness. Besides semi-transparent cupboards, the work counter is a catering unit with water and electricity services visible beneath.

In this conversion of a two-storey apartment on the upper attic floors of a typical Parisian nineteenth-century building on the rue de Rivoli for an architecture critic and her children, the domestic sphere has been treated with a robust functionalism that is unexpected in these rather polite, urbane surroundings. Architect François Roche has used the constraints of a low budget as a springboard for a physically light but conceptually bold intervention that brings light and transparency into the apartment's heart and exploits its position overlooking the Tuileries Gardens. The use of deliberately ordinary cheap industrial materials – sheet plastic for cupboards and plywood for the floor – was a financial necessity, but it underlines the directness of the project.

At entrance level, the living quarters have been simplified to make two interconnecting rooms divided by a load-bearing wall. This wall has been turned into a pivotal feature, serving both spaces. On one side it supports bookcases. On the other, it houses the service facilities, with all the kitchen equipment, groceries and laundry hidden behind semi-transparent plastic doors so that the outlines can just be read as ghostly, refracted images of familiar objects. Different sections of the wall can be opened up as required. The original internal layout of the apartment's small rooms can still be seen mapped out on the ceiling, where vestiges of those walls have been retained to tell the story of a former way of life.

On the bedroom floor, the notion of transparency is repeated, but here it is addressed differently. In an almost Buñuelesque reversal of normal arrangements, bathing, instead of taking place in the privacy of a conventional, opaque bathroom, takes place in a crystal-clear transparent box installed in the bedroom. More than just a flouting of convention that reflects changing sexual boundaries and our increasingly relaxed attitude to nudity, the transparent bathroom cubicle positioned by the window also allows the user to bathe in sunlight and fresh air and makes the bathroom a physically light presence in a comparatively restricted area.

A common problem in the increasingly small spaces characteristic of contemporary apartments, is how to install bathroom and kitchen facilities without dividing the space. Here, despite a limited budget, the conceptual drive of the architect's approach lifts those services out of the ordinary so that they become the focus, even a sort of quiet domestic spectacle.

OPPOSITE AND ABOVE The problem of how to install a bathroom in a bedroom without subdividing the room is resolved here by installing a transparent bathroom cubicle. As well as avoiding a cramped internal bathroom without light or ventilation, this solution playfully reverses our expectations concerning privacy and bathing.

A 60sq.m./650sq.yd. studio is converted
to make a compact apartment with defined work and living areas and a mezzanine sleeping level

The entrance area houses a table, with the kitchen in an alcove leading to the bathroom.

A sitting area is on the far side of the storage wall.

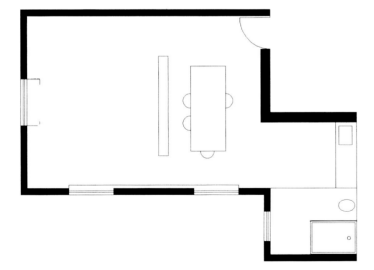

In the central districts of many European cities, pressure on space is such that buildings designed to accommodate large households have been sliced about like savagely dismembered carcasses, to create a warren of small living spaces. This studio flat in a seventeenth-century *hôtel particulier* in the Marais, the aristocratic district of Paris carved into workshops and flats after the Revolution, is typical of this process of dismemberment.

Architectural photographer Christoph Kicherer bought this 60sq. m. (650sq. ft.) space facing onto an internal courtyard for its 3.6m. (12ft.) ceilings and its tall windows. When you reconfigure a space as small as this, the issue isn't so much conversion, as manipulation. Instead of keeping the main room as one, a deep storage wall divides it up. This has proved to be the intervention that makes the flat work. As well as providing a decent amount of storage space – something that is an essential in small-scale accommodation – it creates two distinct living areas: one with a long table for working and eating, the other, a more private sitting area. The bed is slotted into a mezzanine level over the kitchen and the shower and lavatory are housed in a small side room adjoining the kitchen.

The basic pieces of furniture – a long narrow beech table and low bookshelves in wood and polished granite – were commissioned from designer Martin Szekely especially to fit the apartment. In small spaces there is a fine line between the functional and the dysfunctional. Here the attention paid to planning creates a sense of expansiveness that goes far beyond the apartment's actual size.

RIGHT (above) **Essentially one room, the living space is divided by a storage wall to provide a sitting area on one side and an eating and working area on the other.**

RIGHT **The 3.6m. (12ft.) ceiling height gives just enough space above the kitchen to accommodate a mezzanine sleeping level screened by a venetian blind.**

Suburban Britain.

Suburban

The suburban house isn't so much a category of building as a catch-all. It can probably be more easily defined by what it isn't than what it is; and in the context of this book it might seem a curious inclusion. After all, the attraction of suburban housing is its relative freedom. It can even be seen as a *tabula rasa* that can reflect contemporary ideals without reference to past ways of living. After all, it would seem more obvious (and probably more economic) to pull down and replace a suburban house that no longer meets the requirements of contemporary life, than laboriously reshape it.

But as parts of suburbia reach a certain age, buildings as diverse as the turn-of-the-century villa or even the pioneering post-war Californian Case Study houses are absorbed into permanent architectural history and conserved – whether through wish or by law. At the same time, just as suburbia swallows tracts of countryside, in expanding cities such as London, what was once firmly Metroland has been redefined as urban centre and is ruled by its regulations. Thus in suburbia too, conversion, adaptation and all the rigmarole of establishing a pact with the past, have become very real issues. Yet so diverse are suburban houses that it would be slightly ridiculous and indeed pretty much impossible for this chapter to attempt to establish ground rules. Rather, it can only hope to illuminate some of the issues likely to be confronted.

If suburbia isn't defined by building type, what has defined and shaped it is the quest for the space that does not exist in the more densely crowded confines of the city. Suburbia was predicated on the institution of the nuclear family and the single-family dwelling, with the cultural, social and employment advantages of the city as well as the country benefits of fresh air, open space, gardens, peace and privacy. The development of the suburban house in the last hundred years has been shaped by its adaptation to the changing social fabric of the family and changing ideas of its needs.

Although it has its roots in the English Arts and Crafts movement, suburbia, as much of the world has come to know it, took shape in America in the twentieth century. As Californian architect of future suburbias Wes Jones observes, 'For better or for worse, the suburbs are what America came up with when presented with the chance to create its own ideal geography.'

Yet while the suburbs are often disparagingly caricatured as the place where the cultural melting pot is puréed into a puddle of uniform blandness, and where golf and TV dinners stand in for culture, suburbia

at certain times has been the testing ground for new ideas. 'Suburbia is both the test market and final resting place of architectural innovation,' writes Jones. 'The suburbs have been most resistant to change, but [are] also the place where it becomes legitimized when accepted.'

A big part of the attraction of the suburban house is the possibility of outdoor space and the inter-relation between indoors and outdoors, but how these are used is currently being re-evaluated. A defining characteristic of the suburban house is the lot it occupies and the way it sits within it. Commonly as much as one-third of the space is given over to the driveway and front lawn, and to the area between the house and the neighbouring plot, frequently enforced by zoning laws.

The front garden once had a role as a sociable semi-communal space, but today the drive is a show space for a trophy car and the immaculate front lawn is atrophied by lack of use. Front gardens now serve little purpose other than acting as a psychological buffer between neighbours and ensuring the separation of the home from the 'outside' world. This, of course, is largely because, in the search for safety and privacy, the action has shifted to the backyard.

In a modestly ordinary 1920s Los Angeles bungalow transformed by Brian Murphy (pages 146–9), the architect has meticulously reinstated emblems of a disappearing suburban life (laced with irony of course). These include the verandah. Like the front stoop, the verandah once served as a place of connection with the community, but that role evaporated long ago. Here though, by screening the verandah, Murphy has created a semi-protected, semi-private, intermediary indoor/outdoor space that wraps around the house.

In the iconic suburban house Frank Gehry remodelled for his family, the original wooden structure is enveloped in industrial materials, transforming it from a static form to a home that can alter and grow with its inhabitants' needs and changing its relation to the street.

Many of the Case Study houses, the visionary mid-century Program designed to pioneer affordable modern family homes in southern California, renegotiated the relationship between the house and its surroundings. The Program was influenced by changing visions of family life and of course by the glorious Californian sunshine.

Pierre Koenig's Johnson/Riebe house (pages 128–33), a descendant of his Case Study House # 22, reflects the shift in emphasis from street front to a more private outdoor life at the rear, where boundaries dissolve between indoors and outdoors. The street front is deliberately inscrutable, even forbidding, and emphatically shields the interior life of the house. In dramatic contrast, the rear is entirely glass, minimising the division between the interior and the landscape.

With expanding housing needs and the requirements of sustainability forcing us to be more aware of how we use our limited resources, the spatial demands of the suburban way of life are becoming increasingly untenable. As an alternative to wasteful suburban sprawl, Wes Jones has developed a new model for the suburban house. He proposes that the limitlessness of cyberspace could offer possibilities that no longer exist within the limitations of the real world: 'taking the heat off the historic suburban require-

Set amid picket fences and roses, the film *American Beauty* digs behind the immaculate façade of the American suburban way of life to expose it at a time when it is under attack from many quarters.

ment for isolation and separation, the vastness of cyberspace will make up for what might otherwise be felt as spatial deprivation in a denser suburbia.' His alternative suburban home is a utilitarian, almost garage-like structure organised on the lines of the Mediterranean and Arab courtyard house. In the Jones model, the house is internalised, focusing around a private courtyard, and the built space extends to the perimeter of the lot, creating privacy and reducing wasteful side and front yards.

Changing perceptions of privacy have been one of the defining factors in the development of the private house. Curator Terence Riley called the recent show on the avant-garde house at MoMa in New York, 'The Un-Private House', highlighting how changing relations between the home and the outside world are shaping the contemporary house.

In the exhibition, Shigeru Ban's Curtain Wall House, a radical conversion of a traditional family home in a residential district of Tokyo, reflects the client's wish to live in a house 'that is not only constructed with contemporary materials but also evinces the openness and freedom associated with contemporary life'. Here, the living quarters are elevated and treated with the revelatory drama of a stage, their solid walls replaced by giant, billowing white curtains. When the curtains are open, the living floor and bedrooms above are revealed as if boldly as taking the façade off a dolls' house. This effect has been interpreted as a re-working of the Shoji screens that are used to dissolve the boundaries between indoors and out in traditional Japanese homes. Other rooms, including a studio, are in conventionally enclosed spaces at the rear.

The break-up of the nuclear family and the growth in alternative family structures, together with their impact on housing requirements, has been well documented, in Western societies in particular. Like Jones's House, the Oyster House, British architect Nigel Coates's prototype for a suburban house, is designed for flexibility. It can be occupied by a conventional two-parent, two- or three-child family, by two couples or by a group of friends. The crux of this flexibility is the centrally positioned double staircase. This allows separate access from the communal ground floor to the private quarters upstairs, which can be arranged in different configurations ranging from four bedrooms to two self-contained apartments.

American architect Joel Saunders' 'House for a Bachelor' is an extensive conversion of a 1950s house in Minneapolis. Here Saunders rethinks the suburban single-family dwelling to suit the domestic requirements of a single man. This unrealised scheme addresses the issues faced by men and women who live alone or in unconventional relationships. Reversing convention, the house has been excavated to make a subterranean backyard out of sight of the neighbours. This is covered with an astroturf exercise area that flows into the master suite with its bathroom on the scale of a spa. In all these examples, what is apparent is that suburban housing is being challenged by the same needs and desires as other housing types.

A mid-century modern house is
brought up to date to suit the requirements of contemporary living

In contrast to the transparency of the garden façade, the street front is deliberately reserved.

The repositioning of the entrance makes a central hall with long vistas through the house.

The new wing with the children's bedrooms mirrors the master bedroom wing on the other side.

New landscaping makes the house appear to float on a raised platform.

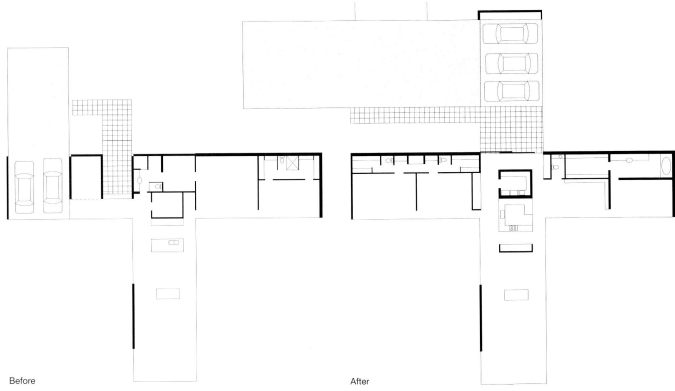

Before

After

Following shortly after Pierre Koenig's Case Study Houses # 21 and # 22, the Johnson/Riebe house 1962/1989 is essentially a Los Angeles suburban house transplanted up the coast to the Eden-like surroundings of the Carmel Valley. It was built for a retired couple, the Johnsons, and after a period of neglect, has been restored and extended by Koenig for the Riebes and their two children.

The Case Study House Program, run by the progressive magazine *Art and Architecture,* aimed to bring family homes that encapsulated the ease of modern life within reach of a larger middle-class audience. It included prototypes by such luminaries as Craig Ellwood, Albert Frey, Charles Eames and Eero Saarinen. According to historian Esther McCoy, 'some of its specific lessons were that a good house could be made of cheap materials, that outdoor living was as valued as indoor spaces, that a dining room was less necessary than two baths and glass walls.' In Koenig's steel and glass pavilions – Case Study Houses # 21 and # 22 – standardised components of the American industrialised landscape were turned into houses of spare and elegant economy, whose transparent flowing living spaces were intended to reflect society's new sense of ease and openness.

Although the currents of social change have been fairly dramatic in the last four decades, the Johnson/Riebe house has stood the test of time remarkably well, both structurally and in terms of the way of life it proposes. The subtle alterations made during its rehabilitation reflect not just the owners' need for additional space, but today's changing requirements and technologies.

As in his earlier Case Study Houses, Koenig moved the emphasis away from the street front to the privacy of the back of the lot. From the road, the low house with its narrow horizontal slit of windows appears dark and slightly forbidding, but once inside, you are drawn towards a transparent prism that seems to dissolve into the landscape. The original house was an L-shape and this has been expanded to make a 'T' with the new arm – on the site of the old carport – housing the two rooms for the children.

Koenig sees his adoption of open-plan living as reflecting the democratic structure of the post-war American family. The main living space is a transparent glass box articulated by the kitchen at one end and a central fireplace that divides the dining area from the open sitting room. In the original plan there were no dividing walls, but among the alterations is a new kitchen, which is no longer entirely open but has a solid storage wall to screen it from the dining area.

By 1962, steel decking spans had doubled in length and Koenig had been able to double his former 3m. (10ft.) building module to 6m. (20 ft.). In the original design, each set of sliding doors was 6m. (20ft.) wide and these opened up so that the walls seems to disappear, to be replaced by the massive canvas of the landscape. For the refurbishment, modern fire regulations required that new windows be a maximum of 1.5m. (5ft.) wide.

In the original plan, the entrance was next to the carport. Now the centrally placed front door leads into an entrance hall that forms a buffer between the living quarters and the bedroom wings. Lined with cupboards fitted with mirrored doors, the 'hall of mirrors' effect is a sharp transition between the taciturn, protective solidity of the front and the disappearing act of the house behind. Rather disconcertingly, the entrances to the bedrooms are concealed in walls of sliding mirrored doors.

One of the main changes of the refurbishment is in the space allotted to bedrooms and bathrooms. The east wing, which previously housed three bedrooms and two bathrooms, is now an extensive master suite consisting of a bedroom and bathroom (considerably enlarged in keeping with contemporary demands) and a study/library wired with computer terminals. This functions as a home office, something that is increasingly a feature of contemporary life. Similarly, the children's rooms in the west wing are equipped with computers.

Another major change is in the landscaping. In the original design, the house was on a low platform, with the lawn sloping gently away. In landscape designer Peter Wilson's remodelling, the house now appears to float on a raised platform, with three steps leading down to the garden.

What is interesting is why the Case Study House Program's enlightened vision of modern living failed to take off in the 1950s. It was Koenig's hope that such models would lead to the mass-production of affordable steel and glass homes. Yet, as the Los Angeles Museum of Contemporary Art's study of the Program reveals, from the 1960s onwards, the Program was sidelined, along with the ideals of Modernism, by the rise of Postmodernism. Now that America is rediscovering its recent past, Modernism of this era has become fashionable again, though it is still confined to a comparatively small audience.

PAGE 129 In mid-century California, the benign climate and post-war prosperity helped foster new developments in the modern house. Koenig uses prefabricated industrial parts to create a domestic architecture of rigorous elegance.

PREVIOUS PAGES The glazed living quarters blurr the distinction between indoors and outdoors so the house effectively becomes a platform in the landscape. The Zen garden is a recent addition, taking the place of a pool that was forbidden by the strict water controls in the Carmel region.

OPPOSITE The new bedroom wing on the left of the picture mirrors the original wing just visible on the other side of the kitchen area.

ABOVE In the renovation, the kitchen area has been partially enclosed by a storage wall.

In a substantial villa, period ornamentation coexists with modern services to make a contemporary family home

Existing architecture provides the ornate framework for modern services.

A series of small rooms has been linked to make a modern kitchen and family room.

Bathroom and dressing room form part of a semi-open-plan master suite.

The basement has been converted to make a pool and fitness centre.

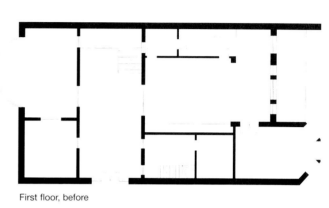

First floor, before

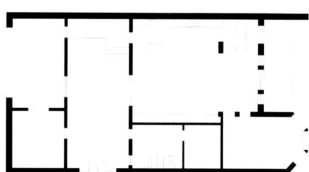

First floor, after

The cohabitation of new technologies with the curlicues and cornices of another age, the search for an equilibrium between old and new – these have become such a normal approach to updating domestic surroundings that they are taken pretty much for granted. But it is tempting to imagine what the original owners of a house like this substantial turn-of-the-century villa in Antwerp would make of its reconfiguration were they to turn up on the doorstep today. Presumably the pallid stripped-down decoration that is such a familiar aspect of today's restrained 'good taste' would look as blanched as a clown's face to someone used to the padded and opulent comfort of the last century. What the original owners would find yet more surprising would be their glimpse of family life a century down the line, and the way the house is inhabited and functions today.

The villa's original hierarchical layout reflected both the formality of its living arrangements, supported by a platoon of servants, and the patriarchal structure of the family. The service rooms and servants' quarters were housed in the basement and upper storey, while the principal entertaining and sleeping floors would have been sandwiched in between. Today, the household is much smaller and the focus has shifted from the parents to family life, and from the formal entertaining rooms to the family room.

In this conversion of a home for her own family, interior designer Nathalie van Reeth has retained elements of the original plan and decoration while making a more open and liveable contemporary home – somewhere 'where you feel there are people in the house'. The change is most radical in those areas that rely on up-to-date services – the kitchen and bathroom. These are rather like modern installations set within the ornate frame of the original house.

While the large first-floor sitting rooms retain their original layout and ornamentation, and with these their sense of formality, a series of smaller rooms has been opened up to accommodate a combined kitchen/living room, treated, by contrast, with functional simplicity. Similarly, in the master suite, increasing emphasis on bathing is reflected in the amount of space dedicated to the bathroom and dressing room.

But equally notable are the new elements that have become part of home life. In this case, both owners sometimes work at home and the positioning of the office next to a sitting room reflects today's increasingly seamless merger of home and work life. Their office may look like a traditional study or library – one of those protected inner sanctums of old where silence reigned – but through new information and communication technologies, it is wired up to the world, breaking the barriers that once divided private from public life.

Another change in today's homes is the emphasis placed on fitness and wellbeing. In this house the basement, which was formerly the kitchen, opens onto the garden and now accommodates a sauna and steam room and a 12m. (40ft.) swimming pool.

PAGE 135 **The view from the master bedroom into the dressing room reveals some of the villa's ornate original plasterwork decoration alongside a rectangular counter that serves as clothes storage.**

OPPOSITE (above and below) **New facilities like the bathroom in the master suite and the pool in the basement are treated with a rigorous, rectilinear simplicity. Levels have been altered so the pool area opens into the garden.**

OVERLEAF **The large kitchen/living room replaces a series of smaller rooms. Rectangular openings linking different areas in the modern parts of the house contrast with the arches and ornamentation of the original structure.**

A house in the suburbs of Paris is reconfigured to make loft-scaled living spaces

The corner house wraps around a courtyard, with living quarters on the first floor and bedroom and studio on the ground floor, with separate access.

The kitchen furniture is over-scaled to fit the large room.

The staircase acts as a hinge between kitchen and living areas.

PAGE 141 **A network of small rooms on the first floor has been cleared away to make an enormous kitchen.**

OPPOSITE **The first floor also houses a large living room with mezzanine.**

BELOW **The staircase acts as a hinge between the two arms of the first floor.**

OVERLEAF **The ground-floor bedroom is effectively a self-contained apartment accessed from the courtyard.**

The Paris home of Li Edelkoort is so decidedly low-key, both in outside appearance and – though in quite a different way – in the treatment of the interior, that it is tempting to link its studiously unpretentious character to the owner's Low Country origins.

The house is situated just outside the *boulevard périphérique*, the ring road that divides the centre of Paris from the suburbs and which, like a protective wrapper, keeps the city centre artificially devoid of much of the messier flotsam of urban life. Unlike, say, the hazy sprawl of London's suburbs, here the divide is so sharp, you would imagine that neighbouring districts on either side of the 'cordon sanitaire' exist in different time zones. One effect of all this is a change in property values so substantial as to make it possible to live comparatively spaciously around the *boulevard périphérique*.

Edlkoort's home is two fairly nondescript suburban houses. When she acquired the property, the houses had already been partially renovated and Edelkoort subsequently worked with Dutch architect Evelyne Merckx to open up and refine the interior.

The unexpected result of the elision is that what were once separate houses now both operate around a central courtyard. But the L-shaped living quarters and terrace on the first floor, and the studio and Edelkoort's bedroom on the ground floor are still accessed separately from the courtyard outside.

The first floor is divided into a sitting area in one arm and an eating area in the other, where the focal point is the kitchen, over-scaled to suit the space. Edelkoort describes the mix of rough-hewn wood and shiny black lacquer as 'techno-primitive'. Upstairs, in the attic level, is a second bedroom and bathroom, and a mezzanine level with separate access.

That Edelkoort chooses to sleep downstairs, on the ground floor, divides the house into day and night apartments in a way that recalls old-fashioned domestic arrangements. In an age where convenience is usually a driving force, it might seem anachronistic to have to go outdoors between floors. Yet it is also possible that, since so much of urban life is rigorously and artificially protected from contact with the elements, such rituals will become more valued as we seek ways of re-establishing roots in the natural environment.

A conversion of a small suburban house exploits the clichés of ''burb' speak

The wrap-around porch creates a semi-private zone between indoors and out.

A freestanding glass panel screens the entrance.

New skylights bring light into the interior of the house.

Openings connect the dining area to the kitchen and living room.

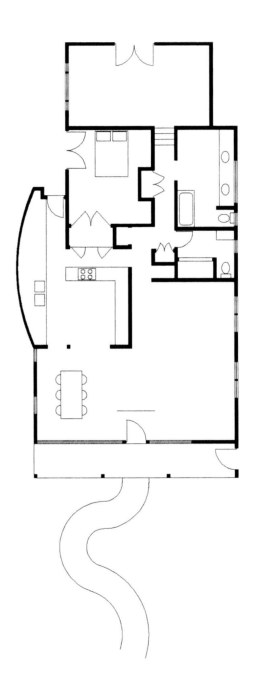

PREVIOUS PAGE **The freestanding glass wall serves as baffle between the front door and the living room.**

ABOVE **Reclaiming the front porch as a living space revives a tradition that has largely disappeared from prosperous suburban life.**

OPPOSITE **At the front of the house, conventional window openings have been replaced by French windows that connect the living area with the porch.**

'There is always something so delightfully real about what is phony here. And something so phony about what is real.' So Noel Coward once observed of Los Angeles. Such ambiguities are part of this rather surreal reincarnation of home-sweet-home suburbia.

Known for his film-set design approach to domestic architecture, Brian Murphy describes this house as a 'little ranch burger' and plays with the pedigree, manipulating the props of ''burb' life – the chain link fence by the sidewalk, the roses, the mail box, the winding path, the white picket fence on the lawn – in a way that seems to border on the disquieting image-making of such film directors as John Walters and David Lynch.

In a typical suburban home the front lawn can often take up as much as a third of the plot. Preserved by planning laws but atrophied through lack of use, front lawns are now often nothing more than a show space for a barely domesticated 4 x 4 vehicle.

Instead, family life has shifted to the relative privacy of the backyard. In this Los Angeles suburban property, Murphy has reinstated the front garden as a focal point, albeit to satirical effect. He has also restored the idea of the verandah as a space that mediates between indoors and outdoors. Enclosed by insect screens, the wrap-around porch here becomes an indoor/outdoor

extension of the living quarters, a semi-private space veiled from the full glare of street life at the front of the house.

Renovated as a part-time home and studio for an artist, the small house that would originally have had a family crammed into a few rooms, is now a generous one-bedroom home with a studio in a lean-to addition at the rear. Instead of completely eradicating the intimate small rooms that would have been a part of the house's original character, Murphy manipulates them. The kitchen and living areas have been linked via openings puncturing the walls, rather than by removing the walls entirely to make a single open sweep. Similarly, although the front door opens directly into the living room, a floor-to-ceiling translucent glass panel acts as a baffle – a modern vestige of an entrance hall. Another intervention are the skylights cut in the roof, which help bring light into the heart of the house and confound one's expectations of a slightly gloomy interior.

In a city where film adds a gloss to fact, Murphy deliberately exploits a set of slightly nostalgic symbols. Suburbia as it hardly still exists is, in his hands, dressed up to within an inch of its life and shrunk to the scale of a crazy-golf course. This is something that could probably only ever happen in La La land.

Why use an architect?

Before choosing an architect, the first question to address is why use an architect at all? With the growth in interior design magazines and books, and with so many television programmes focussing on the home, there has been much hype about a DIY-led approach to home design. Books with chapter titles such as 'How to visualise space like an architect', suggest that anyone can do it on their own. Sometimes this is slightly misleading and sometimes can be even worse.

During a decade of visiting more 'designed' homes than anyone might wish, the dissimilarity between interiors that make a nice photo, and homes that are conducive environments in which to live twenty-four hours a day becomes obvious. When it comes to unlocking the potential of a space rather than merely decorating it, the difference an architect – and not just any architect, but a skilled one – can make, is considerable. A good architect should be able lift a project out of the ordinary, taking design decisions that manage to be both practical and compelling. When refurbishing existing buildings, the constraints can make an architect's skills crucial, since solutions (as some of the projects in this book reveal) may be far from obvious.

However, working with an architect is not just about the design. A building project is a complex process that requires constant monitoring of costs, quality and time. If you use an architect, you are also getting the benefit of that person's considerable training and experience in construction and job management. The architect should be able to explore the most efficient use of the space and consider the building's life cycle, its potential for future change and the costs. On a practical level, an architect can guide you through the complex web of planning regulations and contractual obligations. If required, he or she can also advise on choosing a builder, can administer your contract with the builder and can monitor the construction work through to completion, ensuring it meets the standards required, that it finishes on time and that it does not exceed the contract figure. In some building projects, the role of the architect is also to act as team leader, coordinating engineers, quantity surveyors, builders and subcontractors.

That said, the process of working with an architect requires commitment and communication. Commissioning and realising a domestic project is, effectively, commissioning a bespoke interior and in the best projects, the client as well as the architect invests considerable thought and has a large input.

Given the personal nature of this work, the architect-client relationship can be close and occasionally fraught. There are plenty of historical as well as contemporary tales of combustible falling-outs between architect and client, and the architect is often portrayed as a megalomaniac more interested in fulfilling an artistic vision than accommodating the requirements of the client. Yet if this were generally so, it is unlikely that any architect would find work at all.

Choosing an architect

The next issue is how to find not just an architect, but an architect sympathetic to your thinking and appropriate for the scale and nature of the job.

The easiest way to choose an architect is by finding one whose previous work you like. This is usually done either through recommendation or by researching published work. Professional design and architecture magazines regularly publish surveys of architects practising in different fields and at different budget levels. These publications also promote the work of up-and-coming architects and so they can be a good place to begin your search. Another possible route is to see the work of young architects at college degree shows.

Many architects cut their teeth on domestic work and working with a young architect can be a good way to find someone with imagination and enthusiasm for smaller jobs. It can also give you the satisfaction of helping someone starting out on his or her career. You should, however, bear in mind that a young architect probably has relatively little practical experience of seeing a job through, so you should compensate for this by using an experienced contractor.

The RIBA (Royal Institute of British Architects) can help clients with the process of finding an architect as well as with the procedure for working with one. Their Client's Advisory Service has a database of architects. This gives information on past projects, sectors within which the practice has worked and the range of services offered by the practice. The RIBA also publishes a pamphlet that sets out the basic procedures for finding and working with an architect. The AIA (American Institute of Architects), the RAIA (Royal Australian Institute of Architects) and the New Zealand Institute of Architects can also assist in selecting an appropriate architect. Clients should get in touch with their local chapter (see below).

Once you have contacted an architect or architectural practice, the next step is usually to look at a portfolio of their work, especially projects of a similar scope and scale to your own. You should then visit some of their completed projects. It is worth talking to between three and five architects – enough to see the range of possibilities – before deciding on one you would like to work with. This architect will be someone with whom you feel comfortable and who listens to what you say. You should also respect each other's views. A good way to gauge all this is to see what the architect's approach to your project is and if possible, to visit the site together and discuss his or her initial reactions to it.

At the outset, an architect's design skills may be paramount in a client's mind and the client may give less consideration to technical competence, professionalism and cost, but the RIBA advises, 'Your architects must convince you of both their creativity and ability to get things done'. In order to assess this, as well as visiting some of the architect's previous projects, talk to previous clients about the design process, how the job ran, what they feel about the results and what they might do differently a second time. You should also evaluate how important your project will be to a practice and ask which of their architects will work on your project.

Early in the interview process you should discuss budget, timetable and your expectations, and check that the architect is in agreement with these.

Bear in mind too, that a thoughtful architect is aware that good architecture is the result of a fruitful collaboration between architect and client. He or she will be just as careful about selecting a client as the client will be in choosing an architect.

Appointing an architect

Once you have selected an architect there are a number of different ways in which you can work with them. At the most basic level of involvement, the architect can be hired to consult at an hourly rate. Beyond this, they might be hired to produce a design and see it through planning permission, or at full service, they can see the job through from brief to completion.

Once you have decided on the nature and extent of the working relationship, the next step is to draw up a contract for the work. The nature of this contract varies according to your needs and the law in different countries. The RIBA, AIA and RAIA, as well as similar professional organisations in other countries, all provide guidelines on contracts and publish standard agreements between architect and client. These help establish a basic set of services provided by the architect. Typically, these include: preliminary or schematic design, design development, preparation of construction documents (drawings and specifications), assistance in selecting a contractor and administration of the agreements between you and your builder. Many of the standard agreements provide a menu of additional services the architect can provide, from an economic feasibility study to contract and post-contract administration services.

For example, the RIBA offers a Small Works (SW99) agreement, designed for building projects where the cost is not expected to exceed £150,000. The SW99 consists of a short table of services and a sheet of relevant conditions. It also outlines the procedure for carrying out the work, detailing the stages at which the architect should present a preliminary design scheme for the client's approval, when payment should be made, and so on.

Fees

There is no fixed fee scale and fees can be charged in different ways according to the nature of the scheme and the extent of the architect's involvement. Fees may be charged as a percentage of the construction cost or, depending on the service undertaken, at an hourly rate or as a lump sum. Again the RIBA, AIA and RAIA, as well as similar professional bodies in other countries, can advise you about fees.

Depending on the project, the RIBA advises that architect's fees should come to between 8% and 15% of the total building cost. However, domestic work can be relatively labour-intensive and it is not unusual, to cover the costs on smaller projects, for some architects to charge a higher percentage. At this stage, you should also define reimbursable expenses and should discuss a schedule of payments to help you plan your financial requirements.

Budget

Inevitably, budget will be one of your key considerations and constraints. During your initial discussions with an architect, you should outline the budget you have in mind and see if the architect thinks it is likely to be adequate for the work envisaged.

It is extremely difficult to give a ball-park figure for conversion or refurbishment costs as these can vary dramatically according to the character of the structure, what is being done to it, the level of finish and the type of materials and equipment specified.

In theory, the sky is the limit, although several of the projects in this book are evidence that imaginative design and conceptual clarity can be much more important than a lavish budget. In the case of the London homes by Caruso St John (pages 74–7) and Trevor Horne (pages 38–41), or the Manhattan apartment by Lot/ek (pages 90–93), the success and character of the project are entirely the result of the design vision.

When you are estimating the total budget for your project, in addition to the actual cost of construction, you should take into account other costs such as the fees for architects and other specialist consultants like quantity surveyors (see below), the cost of planning applications, interior decoration, furniture and domestic appliances and, where relevant, the cost of landscape design and other expenses like the cost of providing alternative accommodation for yourself and your family for the duration of the work.

On larger jobs, it may be worth employing a quantity surveyor (QS). The QS is hired by the client to provide an independent assessment of costs and, if required, can provide other services such as monitoring the budget during construction. Your architect will be able to advise on hiring a QS.

Everyone has heard horror stories about architectural projects that run way over budget. Frank Lloyd Wright was famous for squeezing his client's purses and, as his biographer Brendan Gill put it, 'his arithmetic was at the mercy of his desire to create'.

While some circumstances such as unexpected site conditions may be unforeseen, budget problems often stem from not having thought things through at the outset. Clients should be aware that most changes will have budget implications. On the other hand, another reality is that, as a project progresses, understanding increases and the project may change as a result.

For example, it may be necessary to increase certain areas of the budget during the design or construction process. Evaluation of progress at different stages should be used to ensure that there is a continuing consensus on the scope of a project, on quality levels and on construction costs. Some flexibility should be allowed and it is important to add a contingency to the construction cost.

Brief

Before embarking on the preliminary design stage, client and architect should devise and agree the brief. According to the AIA, the owner must provide 'design objectives, constraints and criteria, including space requirements and relationships, flexibility, expandability, special equipment, and site requirements.' Part of the job of the architect is to challenge this and develop a coherent programme. While the architect of a speculative housing scheme or apartment building designs the homes to suit the abstracted needs of an imaginary client or family, if you commission an architect for your home, you are commissioning something that is to be tailored to your personal needs and desires. Therefore the more knowledge the architect can have of how you live and what your requirements are, the more uniquely serviceable the building can be.

But if an architect is to understand your needs, first you must have thought about how you want to live, your practical requirements and how these might change in the future, whether in terms of a change in the size of the household, to accommodate the needs of growing children, or whether you are likely at any time to require space to work at home.

Space planning

If you look at a street of terraced houses at night, the lighting of the rooms often reveals patterns of habitation. In the mid-evening, the lights are usually all downstairs in the basement and on the ground floor, while the part of the house devoted to bedrooms is unlit until bed-time. If the kitchen and family room are in the basement to take advantage of the garden, living rooms on the ground and first floors may be dark much of the time. This gives some idea of how space is utilised in the home and can indicate areas that are under-used.

Some specialists advise carrying out a time/room analysis. While this sounds tedious it can be illuminating. The idea is to analyse how and where you spend time in the home and to use this understanding to prioritise how you allot space. It is done by keeping a record of how much time is spent doing what in which room. Keep a record of an average weekday and also of a day at the weekend, then add up the total hours spent in each room over a week (multiplying the hours of an average weekday by five, and of a weekend day by two) to establish where you spend most and least time.

By rationalising the use of space, you can make the most of the best spaces in the home and minimise spaces that are unused for substantial amounts of time. The time/room analysis process can also help you prioritise how you organise your space and can highlight the possibilities of combining different activities in spaces that are currently under-used. For example, you might put a gym in a spare room, or combine a library and dining area, or you can make a study double as a guest bedroom. It is often suggested that a home office can be hidden away in a box room, in the attic or even tucked under the stairs. But if, in fact, you work a fair amount of the time at home, it makes much more sense to use one of the home's better spaces. On the other hand, you might do away with a separate sitting room if you find that you invariably entertain friends around the kitchen table.

Needs can also be quite individual. During the process of writing a book about bathrooms, I came across a number of people in whose homes the bathroom had risen in importance quite beyond its conventional, utilitarian role. From being marginalised, it had become a centre for domestic activity. One Manhattan architect estimated that, apart from sleeping hours, she spent most of her time at home in the bathroom, getting ready in the morning, relaxing on returning home at the end of the day, then getting ready to go out.

Equally important is for you to consider what the different parts of the building will be like to actually live in. That is why it is a considerable advantage if you can live in a place for some time before you refurbish it as you will then know all its benefits and drawbacks. How natural light works and factors in the immediate environment, such as street noise or noisy neighbours (especially in houses converted into flats, which are often lacking in adequate soundproofing) may not at first be apparent. It is extraordinary that we would not dream of buying a car without first test-driving it yet, although a home is the biggest expenditure for most people, we may have only visited it a handful of times before buying and will rarely have spent a night there.

An alternative approach to tackling such problems is to harness an architect's expertise from the outset. This means choosing an architect before choosing a home and asking the architect to visit and advise on any place you are considering buying.

The design process

First-time clients would do well to get the relevant client packs from professional organisations like the RIBA, AIA and RAIA. These help give an understanding of the nature of the design process and of project management. Your architect should also explain the process and highlight the obligations on both sides.

Standard agreements designate three major design phases and submissions by the architect: schematic design, design development and preparation of construction documents.

Once the brief is established, the usual process is for the architect to produce an outline proposal and develop a schematic design that shows the general arrangement. The owner approves this before moving on to the next stage.

During the design development stage, the architect will produce more detailed designs and outline specifications that list the major materials and finishes. Once the owner has approved the design, the architect prepares detailed drawings and construction specifications. The contractor will use these to establish construction costs and to build the project.

The planning process

You are obliged to comply with legislation governing planning or zoning, building regulations and health and safety, all of which can vary considerably depending on the area, the nature of the building and the work you intend to carry out. Your architect can advise on what sort of consent the work you intend requires and if necessary, can deal with the various authorities on your behalf.

If possible, it is advisable for you or your architect to discuss your intentions with the planners or other relevant authorities at an early stage, so that you can gauge initial reactions before you have gone too far down the line.

If planning is refused, you should learn on what grounds, so that the scheme can be revised or, if it was refused on a technicality, redressed. In certain circumstances it may be possible to persuade the planners to make an exception by arguing a case for an outstanding contemporary design. Again, this is part of the service an architect can provide.

Another contentious area in urban renovations may be conservation and heritage issues and alterations to a listed building or a building within a conservation zone. Your architect will know how to handle these matters or which authorities to consult.

Unless you are experienced in construction matters, once planning has been approved, it is usually worth retaining the architect to administer the construction contract. As the AIA observes, 'When you have taken care to see that a building has been designed as you want you certainly want it built as it was designed . . . Attaining that goal requires considerable, experience, time and effort.'

Hiring the contractor

The process of finding a contractor is similar to that of finding an architect. Usually an architect will suggest one or two companies with which they like to work and you may also have your own contacts or recommendations. As when hiring an architect, it is essential that you have a good relationship with the contractor and faith in his work and standards of construction. In many cases, the homeowner will select from several contractors who have submitted bids or tenders based on the information supplied by the architect. However, the lowest quote is not necessarily the best or most economic in the long term.

Construction

Assuming the architect has been retained, he or she can liaise between client and contractor, can monitor the construction work for its compliance with drawings and specifications, and can approve materials and product samples, review the results of construction tests and inspections, evaluate contractor requests for payments, handle any requests for design changes during construction and administer the start-up and completion process of the project.

Once the building work is completed, the architect will undertake a comprehensive inspection and notify the contractor of any defects to be rectified. It is also usual to agree a review of the building after an agreed period so that any problems that emerge later can be detected and corrected. This gives you some protection against faults developing after occupation.

Sustainability

The re-use of existing buildings can make sense in ecological terms, for recycling can be as validly applied to space as to materials. In *Green Architecture*, Brenda and Robert Vale state as a guiding principle of new green architecture that 'a building should be designed so as to minimise the use of new resources and, at the end of its useful life, to form the resources for new architecture'. This can as usefully be applied to old buildings as it can to new-builds.

However it is sometimes the case that existing structures require such extensive alteration that this outweighs the saving on resources. Minimising intervention is generally an environmentally sound principle, although it may not take into account other important environmental issues such as energy consumption and thermal performance. Yet when it comes to extensively refurbishing old buildings, the choice may have more to do with the building's location than with the actual construction work and the intervention might not make sense in either strict economic or environmental terms.

Useful Addresses

Great Britain

Royal Institute of British Architects
66 Portland Place
London W1N 4AD
Tel. + 44 20 7307 3700

www.riba.net

For information on finding or working with an architect,
contact the RIBA Client's Advisory Service.

America

The American Institute of Architects
1735 New York Avenue NW
Washington, DC 20006
Tel. + 1 202 626 7300

www.aiaonline.com

For information on working with or finding an architect
contact your local chapter of the AIA.

New Zealand

The New Zealand Institute of Architects
72 Dominion Road (suite 1–5)
P.O. Box 2516
Auckland
Tel. + 64 9623 6080

www.nzia.co.nz

Australia

Royal Australian Institute of Architects
www. raia.com.au
For information on working with or finding an architect,
view the Australian Directory of Architects and Building
Designers on the RAIA web site or contact your local
chapter of the AIA.
RAIA New South Wales Chapter
Tel. + 61 2 9356 2955

RAIA Queensland Chapter
Tel. + 61 7 3846 4900

RAIA Western Australia Chapter
Tel. + 61 8 9321 7114

RAIA ACT Chapter
Tel. + 61 2 6273 2929

RAIA Victoria Chapter
Tel. + 61 3 9654 8066

RAIA South Australia Chapter
Tel. + 61 8 8272 7044

RAIA Tasmania Chapter
Tel. + 61 3 6234 5464

RAIA Northern Territory Chapter
Tel. + 61 8 8981 2288

Architects

Adjaye & Russell
24 Sunbury Workshops
Swanfield Street
London E2 7LF
U.K.
Tel. + 44 20 7739 4969
Fax + 44 20 7739 3484

Philippe Boisselier
14 rue de Rivoli
Paris 75004
FRANCE
Tel. + 33 1 42 781 182
Fax + 33 1 42 712 426

Burley Katon Halliday
6a Liverpool Street
Paddington 2021
Sydney N.S.W.
AUSTRALIA
Tel. + 61 29 332 2233
Fax + 61 29 360 2048

Caruso St John Architects
1–3 Coate Street
London E2 9AG
U.K.
Tel. + 44 20 7613 3161
Fax + 44 20 7613 4413

Jo Crépain Architect nv
6 Vlaanderstraat
2000 Antwerpen
BELGIUM
Tel.+ 32 3 213 6161
Fax + 32 3 213 6162

Thomas Croft Architect
9 Ivebury Court
325 Latimer Road
London W10 6RA
U.K.
Tel. + 44 20 8962 0066
Fax + 44 20 8962 0088

Jeff Delsalle
7 Rue Séguier
75006 Paris
FRANCE
Tel. + 33 1 4329 4276
Fax + 33 1 4329 6621

Rodolfo Dordoni
Studio Dordoni
Via Solferino 11,
20121 Milano
ITALY
Tel. and Fax + 39 02 86 6574

Winka Dubbeldam
Archi-tectonics
111 Mercer Street (2nd floor)
New York
NY 10012
U.S.A.
Tel. + 1 212 226 0303
Fax + 1 212 219 3106

Vincent van Duysen Architects
Lombardenvest 24
Antwerpen 2000
BELGIUM
Tel. + 32 3 205 9190
Fax + 32 3 227 2256

Fernlund & Logan Architects
414 Broadway
New York
NY10013
U.S.A.
Tel. + 1 212 925 9628
Fax + 1 212 925 4913

Trevor Horne Architects
14a Clerkenwell Green
London EC1R ODP
U.K.
Tel. + 44 20 7566 0077
Fax + 44 20 7566 0078

Pierre Koenig
12221 Dorothy Street
Los Angeles
CA 90049
U.S.A.
Tel. + 1 310 826 1414
Fax + 1 310 826 3920

Lot/ek
55 Little West 12th St
New York
NY 10014
U.S.A.
Tel. + 1 212 255 9326
Fax + 1 212 255 2988

Brian Murphy
BAM
150 West Channel
Santa Monica
CA 90402
U.S.A.
Tel. + 1 310 459 0955
Fax + 1 310 459 0953

John Pawson
Unit B 70-78 York Way
London N1 9AG
U.K.
Tel. + 44 20 7837 2929
Fax + 44 20 7837 4949

Nathalie van Reeth
9d Leopoldstraat 10,
2000 Antwerpen
BELGIUM
Tel. + 32 3232 4299
Fax + 32 3227 3320

François Roche
45 rue de Belleville
Paris 75019
FRANCE
Tel.+33 1 4206 0669
Fax +33 1 4208 2786

Index

Bibliography

Apartment Stories: City and Home in Nineteenth-Century Paris and London, Sharon Marcus, University of California Press, Berkeley and London, 1999

Architecture Must Burn: A Manifesto for an Architecture Beyond Building, Aaron Betsky and Erik Adigard, Thames & Hudson, London, 2000

Home: A Short History of an Idea, Witold Rybczinski, Viking Penguin, U.S.A., 1986

Loft Living: Culture and Capital in Urban Change, Sharon Zukin, Radius, London, 1988

Lofts, Marcus Field and Mark Irving, Laurence King, London, 1999

Model Apartments: Experimental Domestic Cells, Gustau Gili Galfretti, Editorial Gustavo Gili, Barcelona, 1997

Translations from Drawing to Building and Other Essays, Robin Evans, Architectural Association, London, 1997

The Un-Private House, Terence Riley, Museum of Modern Art, New York, 1999

Acknowledgements

The author and photographer wish to thank:
Andrew Nurnberg; Anne Furniss, Helen Lewis, Hilary Mandleberg and the staff at Quadrille; Nadine Bazar; Richard Blurton and Patrick McKinney; Fiona Dunlop; Paola Morretti.

The author, photographer and publisher would also like to thank all the people who allowed us to photograph their work and in their homes including:
Adjaye & Russell, Philippe Boisselier, Adam Caruso, Jo Crépain, Thomas Croft, Thomas Dane, Jeff Delsalle, Peter Doig, Rodolfo Dordoni, Winka Dubbeldam, Vincent van Duysen, Li Edelkoort, Solweg Fernlund & Neil Logan, Iain Halliday, Trevor Horne, Pierre Koenig, Lot/ek, Yves Marbrier, Jérôme Mazerat, Brian Murphy, Chris Offili, John Pawson, Nathalie van Reeth , Cindy Riebe, François Roche, Yvonne Sporre.

Picture credits

All pictures by Christoph Kicherer except:
14 The National Gallery, London; **15** Rijksmuseum-Stichting, Amsterdam; **16** Geffrye Museum/drawing by John Ronayne; **17** Agence Top/Roland Beaufre (Dennis Severs, London); **18-19** Arcaid/Richard Bryant; **20** ESTO/Peter Aaron; **21** Pierre d'Avoine Architects; **58-59** Cristina Omenetto; **60** Fred W McDarrah; **62** Michael Moran; **63** ESTO/Roberto Schezen; **64-65** Rafael Vargas fotografía; **100-101** Mary Evans Picture Library; **102** Arcaid/Paul Raftery; **103** Lucien Hervé/© FLC/ADAGP, Paris and DACS, London 2000; **104** Gio Ponti Photo Archive; **105** Studio D & L Architects; **122-123** The Independent Picture Syndication/David Rose; **124** Mary Evans Picture Library; **125** Courtesy of Aquarius Picture Library; **126** Julius Shulman; **127 left** Arcaid/Nathalie Topper; **127 right** Hiroyuki Hirai.